KANGAROO
MILLIONAIRE

7 COUNTERINTUITIVE
SECRETS TO SPRINGING AHEAD
IN LIFE AND WEALTH

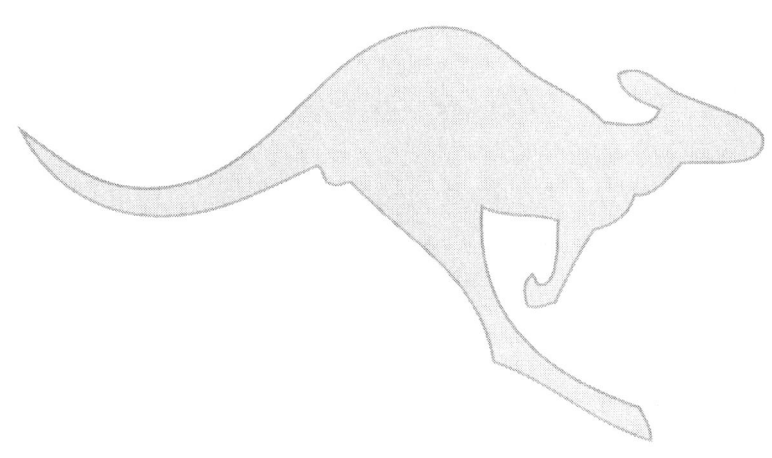

BY MARC HRISKO

Address all inquiries to:

Marc Hrisko

520 W 21st ST G-2

Suite #136

Norfolk, VA 23517

Telephone: 800-589-5410

www.MarcHrisko.com

ISBN-10: 0615247296

ISBN-13: 978-0615247298

Editor: Kym-Maree Hrisko

Every attempt has been made to source all quotes properly

Printed in the United States of America

For additional copies, visit: www.MarcHrisko.com

CONTENTS

ACKNOWLEDGMENTS

There's no such thing as a "self-made millionaire." Neither is there such a thing as a "self-made book." In fact, at the heart of the Kangaroo Millionaire philosophy is the fundamental belief that mentors matter and that numerous people contribute to our success in life and wealth.

In that spirit, I wish to thank a host of individuals without whom this book would have never been written.

First and foremost I wish to thank my "Kangaroo"—the woman who makes everything good in my life even better—Kym-Maree Hrisko. You saw something in me that I did not see in myself. Thank you for opening my eyes and pushing me to climb higher mountains. You define unconditional love; you stand by me and inspire me daily. I love you more than you will ever understand. But I will gladly spend a lifetime trying!

To our two little "joeys," Blake and Austin: thank you for letting your Daddy see the world through your beautiful, innocent eyes. Your love and laughter propel me to work harder and laugh louder. Every second I'm not with you is one second too much.

I love you, sons, with every beat of my heart.

I'm also grateful to Mike and Connie Hrisko. Thank you, Mom and Dad, for teaching me the importance of self-reliance and hard work. Dad, your military service to our country means everything. I am thankful to God that I was blessed with parents who instilled in me the values of selflessness, pride in one's work, honor, and integrity.

My parents also gave me another wonderful gift—a sibling! Julie, I'm grateful for your positive and loving support. I respect and love you. Thank you for always keeping the faith no matter what life throws your way. You are a beautiful blessing, Sis.

A formative part of my professional life was spent alongside some of the most incredible people in the world, my Brother and Sister Firefighters. The attributes and attitudes that undergird the Kangaroo Millionaire mentality were honed and sharpened by working alongside you. Through thick and thin, you taught me what true sacrifice looks like. We held each other's lives in our hands, and in the process you demonstrated time and again what it means to sacrifice for others. Each of you taught me lessons that played a direct role in my success. I thank you from the bottom of my heart.

I also wish to thank those who gave thoughtful and valuable feedback to early drafts of the manuscript, including Rick Watkins, Marian Van Dyke, and Todd King.

Along the way I was also humbled to have been blessed to have some of the most incredible mentors a person could dream of having.

Robert and Kim Kiyosaki: Thank you both for mentoring and teaching me the strategies of success and for allowing me the grand privilege of teaching others your powerful, life-transforming message. Both of you have changed my life—both financially and personally—in more ways than you will ever know. Thank you both for your generosity of spirit and graciousness.

Marshall Sylver: Thank you for teaching me the importance of "Paying It Forward Fast," as well as too many other life and business lessons to list here. You also showed me how to create a life of abundance and prosperity for myself and my family no matter what anybody else or the economy might say. Thank you for showing me how to create my own reality and to utilize the gifts God has blessed me with.

Finally, I wish to thank strategist and friend, Wynton Hall. Never have I met a man who works so hard and so selflessly to maximize the lives and success of his clients. You are a true confidante and friend, and your love for what you do is unsurpassed and infectious to all those around you. May God continue to bless you and your family each new day. Thank you, Wynton, for all you have done and continue to do for Kym, Blake, Austin, and me.

INTRODUCTION

What the Heck is a 'Kangaroo Millionaire'...and How Do I Become One?

I have a confession to make: I married a kangaroo.

Not one of those hippity-hop kinds of kangaroos. No, the kind of "Kangaroo" that made me a millionaire.

I'm referring, of course, to my best friend and inspiration, my wife, Kym, a fiery, brilliant, beautiful Australian who came into my life at the exact moment when I needed her most. She jolted me to spring forward in life and wealth. Well, that's putting it mildly. What she *really* did was kick my butt and get me moving ahead! She motivated me to be more and make more than I ever dreamed I could. And four years later, by my 30th birthday, I was a millionaire.

I owe everything to my "Kangaroo." She pushed me to demand more, to reach higher, and to believe in myself even when others didn't. And along the way I realized that so much of what I thought I knew about achieving millionaire success was incorrect. What I discovered is that millionaire thinking is often counterintuitive. And that's why I wrote this book. I wanted to share the counterintuitive secrets that will spring you ahead in life and wealth.

If you want to be a millionaire you must find your "Kangaroo"—the people, knowledge, and systems that will propel your entrepreneurial instincts forward and send you springing ahead toward millionaire status. You need a Kangaroo. The sooner the better. I was blessed to find my Kangaroo relatively early in my professional career, but when I was starting out, things didn't always look so hopeful.

I was hardly a candidate for entrepreneurial excellence. Growing up, I was always (and still am, I suppose) the black sheep in my family. I love and respect my family deeply, but I never quite fit in. They are all military warriors, doctors, computer programmers, college educated and credentialed. Me? I have a high school diploma and was a firefighter and medic for 10 years. For me, like so many others, high school was an annoying blur of taunting, teasing, and outcast status. Just the normal stuff, really. But at no time would I have been voted the kid most likely to make a million bucks. Ha! I don't even think my classmates would have known my name (or how to spell it) even to put on the ballot!

After school I took pride in fighting fires and protecting lives. Working as a firefighter and medic was a privilege and honor; I'm deeply grateful for the lessons I learned during those 10 years. But all along and at every turn, I always had that nagging feeling inside that I might not be living up to my full potential. I always wondered, "Is this really what God has called you to do forever? Is a $40,000 a year job the highest you can climb?"

Maybe you've asked yourself the same questions. According to the U.S. Census Bureau, the average individual American worker makes $32,140.[1] That's enough to eke out a modest life. And when you compare American prosperity to anywhere else in the world, I think we can all agree that we have much for which we should be grateful. After all, according to the World Bank, 80% of the world's inhabits live on less than $10 a day. So let's be clear: even with the global financial crisis fast afoot, the S&P closing a full 40 percent down for 2008, and jobless rates climbing in 2009 and likely into 2010, most of us live lives the rest of the world can only *dream* of living.[2]

That's why I believe we have an obligation to do more, to make more, to give more, and to share the tools and traits that produce strong financial growth and lasting wealth. And that's the vision my Kangaroo shared with me that led me to make a radical shift in the way I viewed my personal potential. The fact that you're reading this book right now is proof that you're searching for a similar shift in your thinking as well. There are two kinds of people in life: those who control events and those who are controlled by events. I believe you can be the former. I want you to be. The reason I know achieving your entrepreneurial dreams is possible is because I have done it myself. And let me tell you, if I can do it you can too! Heck, you're probably a lot farther down the road than I was when my Kangaroo got me hopping down the path toward millionaire success. But it took her encouragement, her support, and, yes, her kicking my butt to get me up and moving toward living my best life.

So what does it take? What will be required if you truly want to achieve the financial freedom and entrepreneurial satisfaction that comes with making a million dollar income?

Well, for starters, it's not nearly as hard as a lot of people want you to believe it is. And our current financial crisis has created an *INCREDIBLE* ONCE IN A LIFETIME OPPORTUNITY for those wishing to elevate their entrepreneurial game and achieve a 7-figure income within two to three years.

But making your first million will also require knowledge, mentorship, and focus. There is a SYSTEM that leads to millionaire success. But the funny part is that the system rests on extremely counterintuitive principles. Millionaires and billionaires think differently. We view the world—and the entrepreneurial opportunities in it—through a prism that, on the surface, seems strange to the average person. And you see that's why 99.99851% of the planet is not in the millionaires club. They view money and opportunity in ways that shackle success and throw obstacles in front of opportunities.

That's why I wrote this book. Having spent the last several years of my life on stages all across America, coaching my most serious students, and consulting top executives on the proven strategies that build wealth, I decided it was time to share my seven counterintuitive secrets to springing ahead in life and wealth with entrepreneurs, small business owners, and folks who work hard and wonder if there is something more for them and their destinies.

As any of my former students and clients will tell you, I am deeply committed to your success. Why? Because my Kangaroo was deeply committed to my success. I'm passionate about passing along the secrets that lead to massive wealth and freedom. But you've got to want it. You've got to be determined and serious. Quite frankly, you've got to be fed up with living your life at half-speed.

The powerful principles and wealth strategies packed into these pages are transformational. It's not an overstatement to say that they can and will change your life forever if applied. But that's why this book isn't for everyone.

I believe anyone of average intelligence can become a millionaire. So why not YOU?

If you're ready to join the Kangaroo Millionaire Tribe and live the life others dream of, then spring ahead to the next page and keep reading. If not, pass this book along to someone who is. I'm serious. There's no sense wasting your time if you're not serious about success.

Kangaroo Millionaires know deep inside that they are BOUND FOR SUCCESS.

Indeed, it's a scientific fact that it's physically impossible for kangaroos to hop backwards. Instead, they move forward, often at speeds of 40 miles per hour.

So if that's you—a driven, fast-moving, no-looking-back kind of person—then welcome to our tribe. If not, we wish you the best of success in all you do.

Now enough of this chit-chat. We've got YOUR future to build.

So let's get going!

— Marc Hrisko

CHAPTER ONE

IGNORE THE ADVICE OF 99.99851% OF THE PLANET

Over 6.6 Billion People on the Planet Have Never Made a Million Dollars

No enemy is worse than bad advice. —Sophocles

I'm going to put this as gently as I know how to: When it comes to how best to achieve millionaire success, some people don't know what the *heck* they're talking about!

It's true.

All opinions are *not* created equal!

Oh sure, everyone is entitled to their own opinion, as people always say. But that simply means that everyone's "opinion" cancels each other's out. If it's my "opinion" that the stars in the sky are made out of marshmallows, does that mean that stars are now edible?

Of course not.

It means I'm an idiot! Or hungry.

So why, then, do some people take entrepreneurial advice from people who have yet to generate 7-figure incomes in business? Let's get real. Even a person with the best of intentions can destroy your business future by giving you unsound counsel and direction on how to invest your money.

The bottom line is this: People who achieve success in a given discipline are far more reliable resources than those who haven't. Professionals know things that other people don't. It's a fact.

Take, for instance, Tiger Woods. Tiger Woods is arguably the greatest golfer that ever played the game. And that means that Tiger Woods understands things about golf that no one else can comprehend.

For example, the laboratory scientists at Nike's golf club manufacturing facilities created four drivers and wanted to get Tiger Woods's opinion on which one he preferred. After using each club, Woods told the lab scientists, "I like the heavier one." The researchers all scratched their heads and wondered what he was talking about; they had believed that all the clubs weighed the exact same. Now curious, the Nike lab technicians weighed all four clubs. Woods was right. The club he liked did, indeed, weigh more—by the equivalent of two cotton balls.[3]

Think about that. That's how good Tiger Woods is. The man knows and understands things about golf equipment that not even the makers of the equipment understand. How did this happen? Did Tiger Woods just wake up one morning and obtain superhuman powers not available to the rest of the golf-playing world? No.

Instead, Woods and his late father, Earl, and his mother, Kultilda, devoted their lives to perfecting Tiger's golf education. When Woods was only six months old, his mother and father would put him in his baby chair in front of televised golf tournaments, where he would sit in rapt attention for two hours straight. By age three, Tiger shot a 48 on the front nine of a regulation course. Woods's father would often drop his clubs during Tiger's backswing to toughen his concentration and focus. But as strong as Earl Woods was, Tiger's mother was even stronger.

"Old man is soft," Kultida Woods once said of her husband. "He cry. He forgive people. Not me. I don't forgive anybody."[4]

When you consider all of these things, is it any wonder Tiger Woods turned out to be the greatest golfer in history? He was destined for greatness because he and those around him were intensely focused on educating him in the art of achieving excellence. His training produced a reservoir of knowledge. And that's why his body and mind are so finely tuned to golfing perfection that he can grip a club that weighs two cotton balls more than the others and still be able to tell the difference. If you wanted golf advice, whom would you rather get it from? The lab geeks at Nike? Or Tiger Woods?

Obviously, you would want Tiger's advice. And you'd be smart to want Tiger's advice, because Tiger Woods knows how to win. He understands things that others don't and never will.

If you want to be a millionaire, you need to align yourself with entrepreneurial "Tiger Woodses," people who have done what you aspire to do.

There are 6.6 billion people on planet earth, but only 10 million of them are millionaires. Do the math. That means that 99.99851% of the people who live on the planet have never made a million dollars. Does this make them failures? Of course not; that's ridiculous. But it does mean that 99.99851% of the advice you will ever receive about making a million dollars is coming from people who've never done it themselves. Could they get lucky and give you some useful advice? Perhaps. Even a stopped clock is right two times a day. So sure, that's possible.

But the more likely scenario is that they will simply regurgitate something they heard in college, or on TV, or read somewhere that was written by someone who doesn't know what it takes to create massive wealth.

Be Careful Whom You Listen To

Uncle Bob may know a lot about fishing. Aunt Sally may be the world's greatest knitter. Cousin Tommy may be able to barbeque like a champ. But are they millionaires? Have their entrepreneurial decisions resulted in solid and sustained wealth-building? OK then. So why would you listen to them lecture you about your business ideas? Worse, why would you let them ridicule your dreams? Why would you take advice on how to become a millionaire from anyone who hadn't already achieved millionaire status if your goal is...well, achieving millionaire status?!

It doesn't make sense.

Now don't get me wrong. Uncle Bob, Aunt Sally, and Cousin Tommy are probably fine and decent people with a lot of wisdom to share. But let's get real: they haven't achieved the goal you're after. They haven't bounced down the Kangaroo Millionaire path. Does that make them bad people? Absolutely not! Does that make them less likely to know the blueprint for 7-figure success? You better believe it.

I know I'm being blunt here, but I have to be. Think of all that's at stake: your children's future, your family's home, the time you are able to spend with your family, the time you are able to spend serving others and doing the things you love (hopefully these are one in the same). All of that and more are riding on whom you listen to for advice. That's why you can't afford to rely on the entrepreneurial and investing advice from folks who, despite their best intentions, have never played the game at the highest levels and won.

Here's how seriously I take this principle. Whenever I meet with a potential financial advisor, say, a stock broker for instance, the very first question I ask them is this: "Did you make a million dollars last year?"

Blunt? Yes. Important to ask? You're darn right it is!

Now, I know what you may be thinking, you may be saying to yourself, "Oh, I don't think I could ever be that forceful and 'in your face' to someone I just met. I'd feel rude." Here's what I say to that: Rude? Are you kidding me? You're about to place a large chunk of your financial fate into a total stranger's hands, and you're not going to find out first whether she or he is a good steward of their own money? Heck, the only thing that's "rude" about that mentality is what it means for your children and your family's future. Now *that's* rude!

If someone comes to you promising to help you build massive and sustainable wealth, then surely they shouldn't be embarrassed or offended when someone wants to know about their personal wealth track record. If they do, run in the other direction. That's like a professional baseball pitcher getting offended when a new team looks up his pitching statistics before deciding whether they want to sign him to their team. If the pitcher is good at what he does, he will *want* people to look up his track record!

When it comes to advice, so often we hear what we want to hear and forget the rest. It sort of reminds me of the story of the 92-year old man who went to the doctor to get a physical. A few days later the doctor saw the man walking down the street with a gorgeous young lady on his arm and a big smile on his face.

> *Excellence is not an exception, it is a prevailing attitude.* — General Colin Powell

The doctor went up to the man and said, "Well, it looks to me that things are going really well for you. What did you do?"

The man replied, "Just following your advice, Doctor. Get a hot momma and be cheerful."

"I didn't say that," the doctor said. "I said you've got a heart murmur and be careful."

The lesson? Listen to what you NEED TO HEAR, not what you WANT to hear!

Once you understand how few people on planet earth are truly millionaires, it will change the way you think about the entrepreneurial advice you've received throughout your life. With all due respect to those who gave you that advice, most of them have never achieved 7-figure success in their business ventures. Kangaroo Millionaires understand the power and importance of the previous sentence. It transforms the choices they make and the individuals they align themselves with.

Be smart.

Be wise about who you listen to.

Align yourself with those who've done what you seek to do.

TAKE ACTION NOW!

- Identify the person in your social sphere who has achieved the greatest success in business and take them out to lunch. Then ask them questions and shut up and listen to what they say. Their wisdom is worth its weight in gold.

- Hop on to your Facebook, MySpace, LinkedIn, or other social networking sites and "friend" 5 successful individuals whom you respect. Seeing their image on your "friends" list will remind you whom you should listen to.

• Take out a piece of paper and write down the entrepreneurial and financial advice you've received and implemented up to this point. If you don't have a 7-figure bank account, light a match and burn the paper. Clearly that advice hasn't worked.

• Put yourself directly inside the orbit of small business owners by joining *Entrepreneur* magazine's own social networking site for small business owners (http://econnect.entrepreneur.com/) Membership is FREE!

Millionaire is a State of Mind

Millionaires and billionaires see the world differently. Oh sure, we want the same things you want: more time with our families; the freedom to volunteer our time and talents to the causes we believe in; the ability to provide a better, more stable life for our children and spouses; and the freedom to enjoy the world and all God's creation. But we don't see opportunity as something that seizes us but rather as something that we must seize ourselves. Once we find our opportunity, we take advantage of it to the fullest—and right away.

That reminds me of the great story about the three men traveling across the desert by camel on a moonless night when a commanding voice from the darkness brought them to a startled halt.

"Dismount at once," said the booming voice, "and fill your pockets with the pebbles scattered all around you. Do it immediately!"

The men quickly and fearfully did as they'd been told.

When they remounted their camels, the voice continued, "Tomorrow morning you will be both glad and sad about what you have done tonight. Now continue with your journey."

When the sun rose, the men looked in their pockets and were amazed that they were not filled with pebbles but diamonds.

But as the voice had warned, they were both happy and sad. Happy that the pebbles turned out to be diamonds, but sad that they had not taken more.

Kangaroo Millionaires know how to sense when they have wandered into a field of diamonds. And when they do, they pitch a tent, set up camp, and they don't stop until they've harvested all the opportunities they can.

Along with sensing opportunity comes rejecting the victim mentality that often comes from those individuals who have never achieved financial freedom. Successful entrepreneurs aren't interested in excuses, whining, self-pity, or a victimhood mentality. In fact, Kangaroo Millionaires reject these mental frameworks with a vengeance. They are optimistic go-getters who would rather roll up their sleeves and make things happen than to sit around daydreaming all day about some mythical fantasy lifestyle. The secret is to make your dreams a reality, and that means having the right mentality! It also means blocking out the people who are secretly rooting for your failure. But bounding ahead means fixing your mind on an unrelenting focus on using the gifts God has given you to their fullest potential.

TAKE ACTION NOW!

• For the next 24 hours, refuse to make any excuses for anything. Take complete responsibility for everything—no matter whether it was your fault or not. That's the mindset of a leader. That's the mindset of a Kangaroo Millionaire.

• Begin each day with 15 minutes of quiet time. Read a devotional or some form of inspirational reading that will elevate your spirit. When I'm traveling and delivering seminars, my wife will send me a morning Bible verse or line of inspiration on my BlackBerry just before I hit the stage. It works wonders for my mindset and energy.

• Enforce a zero tolerance policy for whining and blame shifting among those on your team.

Remove the "Crabs" from the Bucket

Comedian Chris Rock has a hilarious routine he does about the "crabs in the bucket" mentality. Rock says that any time a person tries to climb higher than their circumstances and surroundings, critics gather around him or her like crabs in a bucket and try to pull them back down. When I set out to achieve entrepreneurial success, I had several people tell me I was too stupid to be able to achieve my goal. Sadly, some of those negative voices even included some of the people closest to me. Jealousy and envy are powerful and destructive forces. But you can't let them stop you. You *must* not let them stop you.

You have to block out the negative voices and naysayers. Thankfully, I had my wife, my Kangaroo Millionaire, supporting me every step of the way. She had come from a family of driven, ambitious Aussies who took the bull by the horns and never gave in to the negative and defeatist mindset that grips so many people. But sadly, most people don't have this kind of support network or access to high-performing and successful people. Indeed, many people—maybe even you—have suffered from friends and/or family members who tore down their dreams and mocked their ambition. It's not that these folks are necessarily evil people. It's just that they see someone else rising above and taking the kinds of risks they wish they had the courage and drive to take. Your vision and vigor intimidate them, and they don't know how else to respond other than to open up their "pincers" and try to pull you back down into the bucket. Don't let them. Overcome their objections. Heck, they'll thank you for it when you become a millionaire, because you'll buy them nicer Christmas gifts!

> *Positive thinking will let you do everything better than negative thinking will.* — Zig Ziglar

The key is to seek out mentors and a support network that create a culture of positivity. Now, I'm not of the school of thought that says, "Just think positively and you'll make buckets of money." That's not how it works. You have to understand the systems of wealth creation; creating a positive "playground" for your ideas and work is critical.

One person who "gets" that is Stacey King. He's the kind of guy you want on your team—extremely positive. Stacey King was a rookie NBA basketball player with the Chicago Bulls during Michael Jordan's tenure there. King said he would never forget one of his first games playing alongside the legendary Michael Jordan.

Jordan led the Bulls to victory that game when he scored an amazing 69 points. King? He scored just one single point at the foul line.

After the game, a reporter asked Stacey King for his reaction to the Bulls' victory, and he replied, "I'll always remember this as the night Michael Jordan and I combined for 70 points."

Ha! You have to love a guy with that kind of positive mindset! Learn to find the good in life and life will find the good in you.

TAKE ACTION NOW!

- Whip out your cell phone and delete the numbers of those people who tear you down or put you in a negative mindset. I'm serious. Do it now. They are holding you back from bouncing ahead.

- Never hesitate to stop someone mid-sentence if they are spouting defeatist drivel. Simply say, "I'm sorry, let me cut you off right there. I don't share your pessimism and I really don't see the point in spreading it."

- When you get an email brimming with gossip or negativity, zap it into the delete file. Life's too short for that silliness. Plus, emails get forwarded. Elevate your standards and your mind and leave that junk behind.

- Ignore the naysayers. Their motives are not pure, nor do they have your best interests at heart. Their envy and jealousy have gotten the best of them. They are to be pitied. But don't let them waste your time. You've got goals to accomplish.

Become an Action Hero

One of the biggest keys to 7-figure success that 99.99851% of the world fails to understand is the importance of *speed of implementation*. And again, this all deals with the way you THINK about entrepreneurial opportunities and strategies. You have to become what I like to call an "Action Hero," meaning a person who refuses to hesitate when massive opportunity presents itself. The deciding factor between those who achieve and those who fail is often little more than the speed with which they implement a winning strategy or seize upon the golden ring when it appears. This means learning when to take calculated, smart risks and knowing when to walk away or ignore the advice of the 99.99851% people who, despite the best of intentions, haven't the slightest clue about how responsibly and effectively to generate wealth that lasts. Most people have difficulty knowing when to seize an investment opportunity and when they should pass it up.

When I'm on stage delivering one of my seminars I sometimes demonstrate this point by telling the crowd that in my pocket I have something that will GUARANTEE that they will instantly make $200 in cash, and that all they have to do to retrieve it is be the first person to give me $100. Some people squirm as they go back and forth in their minds over whether to take the offer. Others nervously cover their wallets or clutch their purses, unwilling to part ways with the $100 they have versus the $200 I'm guaranteeing them. But the future successful entrepreneurs in the crowd—the Kangaroo Millionaires—bound as fast as they can to try and be the first person to the front of the room. All they needed was the nudge from me and the opportunity to win. And when they do, they find that the SPEED with which they acted is rewarded, because I reach down into my pocket, snap off two $100 bills from my money clip, and send that person back to their seat having made an easy chunk of change.

The lesson: millionaires and billionaires are Action Heroes. They leap into action when they see the window of opportunity right in front of them. They train their minds to know that speed equals success. The sooner you implement the right business strategies, the sooner your venture or investment can take flight. As is often said, millionaires are risk-takers. They realize that the status quo will get you nowhere.

You have to be willing to make things happen. After all, there is a reason the word "Action" precedes "Hero." You have to take the former to become the latter.

> *Your time is limited, so don't waste it living someone else's life. Don't be trapped by dogma—which is living with the results of other people's thinking. Don't let the noise of other's opinions drown out your own inner voice. And most important, have the courage to follow your heart and intuition. They somehow already know what you truly want to become. Everything else is secondary.* — Steve Jobs

So what action should you take to become a Kangaroo Millionaire, someone who only moves forward on their path to financial freedom and a better life? The answer might surprise you: Quit your job. Not right this second. But eventually, that has got to be your biggest goal if you're serious about achieving millionaire status. Not to be stuck in the "rat race," as Robert Kiyosaki calls it, is your ultimate objective. That means learning the wealth strategies that allow you to set up passive streams of income that allow you to have the financial flexibility to live life on your terms, not your boss's. As Marshall Sylver likes to say, J-O-B stands for "Just Over Broke!"

It's true.

Entrepreneurs account for the overwhelming majority of millionaires. In his classic and intriguing study of American millionaires, Dr. Thomas J. Stanley found that although the self-employed account for less than 20% of the total workforce, a whopping two-thirds of all American millionaires are self-employed entrepreneurs who own their own businesses.[5] Now what does that tell you? That tells you that your mindset should be focused like a laser beam on becoming an entrepreneur, creating a thriving business, and quitting your J-O-B forever.

I'm dead serious.

Pursuing the path of entrepreneurship offers you the highest percentage odds to millionaire wealth.

"But hold on a second," you say. "Why are the overwhelming majority of millionaires business owners? Aren't there other ways to generate massive wealth?" Sure. There are. But unless you can throw a football 60 yards with pinpoint accuracy, sing high notes that can shatter glass, or can write literature that gives Hemingway and Faulkner a run for their money, your highest percentage odds of success for making and sustaining a seven-figure income is found in the world of entrepreneurship.

Stop and think about it.

> *The pessimist sees the difficulty in every opportunity; the optimist sees the opportunity in every difficulty.*
> — Winston Churchill

Businesses turn profits by keeping costs fixed and preferably low. And one of the

biggest costs, of course, is labor. That means that there is generally a fixed "ceiling" in

place above which most positions will never pay. For instance, if you are a manager of a McDonald's restaurant, no matter how spectacular you are at managing your team, there is a predetermined, fixed dollar amount over which you are unlikely ever to earn. And trust me, that number is nowhere *near* seven figures! In fact, it's unlikely that number will ever break six figures.

That means you have to take the mental leap from thinking like an employee to thinking like a business owner and entrepreneur. Only then will you ever be able to achieve millionaire status. You have to be an Action Hero who's willing to take the steps necessary to change your reality and learn and master a new and, yes, *counterintuitive* way of thinking.

So what are you waiting for?

Be the hero.

Spring into action!

TAKE ACTION NOW!

- Right now go to www.GoDaddy.com and reserve a few website domains of potential business names you like. If you don't already own your name.com, start with that if it's still available. Registering a domain costs less than lunch at Taco Bell (usually under $10). Yet the simple act of "reserving" your future business will motivate you and get your Kangaroo Millionaire mind hopping in the right direction.

- Go to www.VistaPrints.com and order FREE business cards with a possible name for your business, your name, and the word "Owner" underneath it. Then put the card in your wallet so that you see it daily. If you never use the cards or settle on a different name for your business, who cares? It's the mindset shift we're after the most, the rest will follow.

• Write your two week notice for your present job. You're not going to quit tomorrow, so calm down! But here again, the simple act of preserving on paper your future goal will slingshot your mind into the future and get you focused on becoming a business owner, which, as we've seen, is the highest percentage path to millionaire wealth.

Your Mentor's Values Matter

Imagine how different history would have been if Josef Stalin's mentor had been the great nonviolence advocate and Indian freedom leader Mahatma Gandhi instead of Vladimir Lenin, Russia's first communist dictator. How might Osama bin Laden have turned out had he been mentored by the likes of a Dr. Martin Luther King, Jr., early in his life? What would have become of serial killers had men and women of integrity intervened early in their lives and instilled the kinds of enduring values that shape a person's character and destiny, values like honesty, trustworthiness, hard work, fairness, generosity, decency, concern for others?

We can never really know for sure, but there's a likely chance that it would have made a difference.

You need to ignore the advice of people who don't share your values. That doesn't mean you need to be judgmental;

rather, it means you need to be wise about the kinds of people you take counsel and mentorship from.

I have been blessed with wonderful mentors and coaches over the years. Even today I continue to surround myself with the kinds of entrepreneurs, thinkers, authors, and fellow National Speakers Association (NSA) speakers whom I feel I can grow and learn from.

> As iron sharpens iron, so one man sharpens another. — Proverbs 27:17

It's been said that you are the average of the five people you spend most of your time with. There's a lot of truth in that. After all, why do we work so hard to get our children to choose the right friends? It's because we know that even the strongest child can still get caught in the crossfire of a bad kid's shenanigans.

Surround yourself with the kinds of people you wish to become. Your learning should never stop. You must always be furthering your education and improving your understanding of the systems and strategies that build and grow wealth. Sharpening your skills means choosing the right mentors and coaches. And that's why I only partner with people whose values lead them to pursue the kinds of ethical decisions I can support. Ignore everyone else, no matter how much money they claim they can make you. After all, if you can't trust their values, how can you trust their claims?

Case in point: Wall Street mega-titan Bernard Madoff, the man charged with being responsible for the biggest financial scandal in the history of the markets. In January 2009, the $50 billion dollar scam bloodied investors by creating fake investment returns. As Madoff confessed, it was "all one great big lie." Even Hollywood director Steven Spielberg's holdings were hurt by the scandal. But worst of all, numerous charities that depended on Madoff and his clientele for their philanthropic support were destroyed overnight.

"Sometimes we have seen this wrongdoing happen, and it cuts into endowment funds. But I have been working here for 10 years and I haven't seen a situation where organizations simply disappeared," said Michael Nilsen, a senior director at the Association of Fundraising Professionals.[6]

In business, values have consequences. If a person's only motivation is making millions, then they will justify decisions and actions that are unethical and possibly even illegal. Ignore these individuals. Like Bernard Madoff, they may build a golden castle all the way up to the sky, only to have it come crashing down all around them and everyone around them.

When looking for your Kangaroo, find a mentor who shares a commitment to the values that define you and then build your power team.

TAKE ACTION NOW!

- Identify your "non-negotiable" business values. Then stick to them. Always.

• Be shrewd and discerning about the individuals with whom you create alliances. Your reputation is your greatest asset. Don't squander it on someone unworthy of your time, talents, and trust.

• Do your due diligence. Check people out. There are numerous online sites that will ethically and legally run background checks on individuals.

• Always trust your gut. If you get a bad vibe from a potential mentor or business partner, trust it. God gave you instincts for a reason. Use them.

CHAPTER TWO

DEBT ISN'T ALL BAD

"Debt" Can Make You a Millionaire

A national debt, if it is not excessive, will be to us a national blessing. —Alexander Hamilton

What do you call a man who is $30 million dollars in debt?

Really, really, really rich, that's what!

Just ask Felix Dennis, one of the richest men in all of Great Britain. How rich? Well, let's put it this way. Dennis says he has so much money he's really not sure what he's worth. But the figure could be as high as $900 million. That's more money than the GDP of some small countries. He owns five homes, three estates, fancy cars, private jets, thousands of acres of land, expensive art, private wine cellars bulging with bottles of expensive spirits, has chauffeurs, housekeepers, armies of financial and legal advisors...and debt. Lots and lots of debt.

"Around $30 million of debt," says Dennis. "Rich people always have a certain degree of debt. Apparently it helps to reduce taxes—but I'm not so hot on the bean-counting side.

In fact, I still haven't quite gotten the hand of a balance sheet. Amortization always floors me."[7]

Felix Dennis made his fortunes in magazine publishing. As a stellar entrepreneur, Dennis understands what few others do: There's a major difference between "good" debt and "bad" debt. Before we distinguish between the two, however, let's face some facts.

You're Already "In Debt."
But Is Your Debt Making You Millions?

If you have a mortgage payment, you're in debt. If you have college loans, you're in debt. If you have a car payment, you're in debt. If you have a child about to enter college, you're about to be in major league debt…assuming they don't have a full-ride academic or athletic scholarship.

The point is, "debt" is something most people are already in and yet pretend not to be. Given the current shockwaves going through the global financial markets, most folks are especially sensitive to the notion that they are in debt. But the simple fact is that a liability is a liability, plain and simple. And anything that's an expense is, in financial terms, a liability.

"Oh no," most people say, "those things you mentioned like a home, a car, a student loan…those aren't 'debt', you see. No, those are INVESTMENTS."

Ahhhh….I see. So if it's something you want (house, car, etc.), then it's an "investment." But if it's something you don't necessarily want or think you need, then—and ONLY then—is it to be considered a "debt?!"

How convenient!

You see, a house or education CAN BE investments. But they are a form of "debt" (liability) nonetheless, at least insofar as your bank is concerned. The question isn't whether you have debt, the question is whether your debt produces massive profits. So, as an entrepreneur trying to determine which investments or markets to enter, how do you determine what constitutes "good" debt versus "bad" debt?

"Good debt," says Eric Gelb, CEO of Gateway Financial Advisors, "is investment debt that creates value; for example, student loans, real-estate loans, home mortgages and business loans."[8]

NY Times bestselling financial author, David Bach, agrees.

"Home values have increased an average of 6.5%, per year over the past 30 years," says Bach. "So when you borrow to buy a home, chances are that's good debt. You'll build value."

Bach points to some staggering statistics to drive home his point.

"The average renter has a median net worth of $4,000, and the average homeowner has a median net worth of about $150,000."[9]

Real estate is where I made my millions, and I strongly and passionately encourage others to do the same. Why? Well, because the numbers don't lie. Real estate remains one of the most powerful vehicles for wealth creation. As President John Adams once famously said, "I had heard my father say that he never knew a piece of land (to) run away or break." This is especially true RIGHT NOW! Adams was right; real estate is an outstanding investment vehicle. In the wake of the global financial meltdown, and the bursting of the housing bubble, real estate opportunities are MASSIVE! Like the old Irish proverb says, "Everyone is foolish until he buys land."

> *The best investment on earth is earth.*
> *—Louis J. Glickman*

Tomorrow's class of millionaires and billionaires will be minted beginning in 2009. Those who seized the real estate bargain basement opportunities that are everywhere will be handsomely rewarded. The bigger point, though, is that good debt refers to those investments with strong and predictable patterns of appreciation. Conversely, bad debt is anything that will result in high levels of depreciation.

Entrepreneurs understand that "debt" can make you millions IF—and this is an important "if"—you take on good debt. As a January 2009 article in CNN Money notes, "Debt is not always a bad thing. In fact, there are instances where the leveraging power of a loan actually helps put you in a better overall financial position."[10]

TAKE ACTION NOW!

- Take a long hard look at where you're spending your money. Does your spending go toward resources or investments that are likely to produce wealth or squelch it? Go look at how many songs are under your "Purchased" header on your iTunes account. Calculate how much money you blow on fast food and Starbucks. It adds up. But is that the kind of spending likely to produce wealth? Or would those funds have been better spent on advancing your entrepreneurial path toward becoming a Kangaroo Millionaire? I think we both know the answer.

• Understand that debt can be a tool used to leverage Other People's Money (OPM) to advance your entrepreneurial endeavors. Do you think Donald Trump cuts a check from his own personal checking account every time he builds a new building? Heck no! He leverages debt and comes out the big winner.

• Resist the temptation to demonize "debt" broadly defined. I'm not talking about the kind of debt the Bible and other sacred texts warn against that is incurred by immoral or illegal means. In fact, most houses of worship would never get built (not to speak of the homes of religious leaders) were it not for their willingness to take loans.

• So-called "good debt" is akin to what successful entrepreneurs call "calculated risk-taking." If you know that there are high odds that your leveraged debt will produce sizable profits, you would be unwise not to capitalize through some form of loan and turn it into a profitable investment.

Show People ROI & the Rest is History

It's all about ROI.

If you believe that a $150,000 degree from Harvard University, plus the years of lost wages and work history it will take you to gain that diploma, will yield you even greater returns, then an Ivy League investment may be a wise one. But here again, you can't just stop there. You have to go deeper and ask yourself whether that investment makes sense *relative to other options*. That question is at the heart and soul of your return on investment (ROI).

There are a zillion ways to make money, but only a handful of them will truly yield a million dollars. Why? Well, because the return on investment of, say, selling snow cones can only be as high as the cost of the unit you're selling (in this case, snow cones). Even if you were somehow making one dollar off of each snow cone you sold, you'd still have to move 1,000,000 snow cones.

That's a lot of shaved ice and sugar water!

This means wannabe millionaires need business and investment strategies that bring a fat payday for each transaction. And in an optimal scenario, we want to be involved in an industry where we can replicate the process quickly and without a lot of lost time and revenue that also keeps our overhead low.

But there's another important ROI principle Kangaroo Millionaires understand that most others do not. And this principle should drive your sales strategy.

> *An investment in knowledge always pays the best dividend.* —Benjamin Franklin

Let me explain.

Entrepreneurs sell. And selling is about showing prospects the value that your good or service can bring them. At its root, selling is about showing others how you want to serve *them* and meet *their* needs and desires. This means you have to demonstrate, in clear and dramatic fashion, how an investment in your good or service is GUARANTEED to produce powerful and positive outcomes. The best way to do this is to monetize the exact value they will receive. The effect you must leave in their minds should go something like this, "Well, since you put it like that, this is really a no-brainer. Even if I only received half of the results you promise, I'd still be coming out majorly ahead. So, yeah, let's go ahead and move forward. How can I get in on this? Sign me up for your program!"

Let's take a real example from a student of mine. If you pay close attention, the next few pages will teach you a principle that very well could transform your entire business forever.

I'm not joking.

Pay *very, very, very* careful attention to what I'm about to share with you.

The strategic advice embedded in the next few pages may bring you a 1,362% return on your investment in this book.

At least, that's what it brought him. I'm probably an idiot for giving away such a powerful sales strategy for so little.

But what can I say?

I'm generous to a fault and am in a giving mood.

Okay, here goes:

My student is a renowned bestselling author. There's a good chance you've read his work before. He's been published in every major newspaper, is on TV often, and has written bestselling books. Well, anyway, he came to me because he wanted to begin getting into writing content for audio courses. After attending one of my speeches he approached me and said, "Marc, I love writing books, but I really think I could expand what I do into helping leaders create 6-disc CD courses and home study courses. But I don't know the first thing about sales or 'pitching' and I don't like feeling cheesy or slimy about selling things."

"Hold on right there a second," I interrupted. "What's cheesy about wanting to serve other people by providing them with superior knowledge that can change their businesses and lives?" I asked.

"Well…uh…um…," he muttered.

"Exactly. Nothing!" I said.

He nodded in agreement.

"So now that you have the right servant sales mindset, let's talk about ROI."

"Well that's the thing," he said, "I'm a writer, a literary type, so I don't really know much about numbers and all that."

"Fair enough," I said. "But you do know something about keeping a person's attention. After all, that's what great writers do. You grab people's attention by telling a powerful story that makes them want to flip the page," I explained.

"That's true. You're right, Marc."

"I know I'm right. That's why you're going to take the $10,000 piece of entrepreneurial advice I'm about to give you for free," I said.

He leaned in closer. As it turned out, the advice ended up being worth literally three times that amount. But neither of us knew it at the time.

"Here's what you're going to do," I explained. "Right now I want you to tell me how much the average price most speakers would sell a premium 6-disc comprehensive home study course for."

"Oh, I don't know," he said. "It could easily go for $497, I suppose."

"Okay," I said. "Let's imagine that it was a really, really great course. I mean, the kind of content that could rocket people to the next level and create massive success for their businesses and lives. Truly tremendous content with no fluff or filler. But let's imagine that instead of the $497 that it was truly worth, let's say it only cost $297. Now, how much money would you charge a leader to help her or him develop such a product?"

"Well, Marc, you see, that's the problem. When I write my books I usually get about $30,000 a book. But there's no way in the *world* I could ever go up to someone and say, 'Hey, I want to create an audio course for you, but it's going to cost you $30,000.' I mean, they'd die of sticker shock, Marc!"

"Really?" I said. "Is that seriously what you believe?! Have you learned nothing from me?!" I scolded.

He looked away.

"Look," I said. "First of all, $30,000 is nothing. It's chump change. And the truth is that if you are willing to make a 6-disc audio product for someone for only $30,000, that person would be a moron not to take you up on it."

"I'm sorry, Marc," he said quizzically. "I'm not following your logic."

"I know you're not," I said. "Watch this."

I then pulled out a piece of a paper and scribbled out the following ROI monetization:

Creation of 6-Disc Audio Home Study **for Content Creation**	**Course** **$30,000**
	--Divided By--
6-Disc Audio Home Study Course— Selling Price	**$297**
Units Needed to be Sold to Recoup Investment:	**101 Units**

"There's your pitch," I told him while tearing the sheet off the legal pad and handing it to him. "Any businessperson with a brain is going to *lunge* at that offer. All they have to do is move 101 units of their life-transforming content at the reduced price of $297 and they will have recouped their costs instantly. Heck, they'll probably do that the very first time they speak to their next audience. After all, who in their right mind wouldn't buy a 6-disc study at home course for $297 if they knew it could produce a huge benefit to their lives and businesses? So we know that people are going to be buying the audio course in droves!"

"Well, yeah," he said. "I guess that's kind of a no-brainer."

"Of course it is. But do you realize what that means for your potential client?" I asked. "It means that their return on investment (ROI) will be recouped almost the *instant* they receive the product you're going to create for them! It means that all they have to do is sell a measly 101 units of their life-changing audio course and they will have INSTANTLY recovered their initial investment. Better still, from that point forward, every single unit they sell will be pure profit in their pocket!"

"Wow!" he said. "I guess I never thought of it quite like that."

> *Quality in a product or service is not what the supplier puts in. It is what the customer gets out and is willing to pay for. A product is not quality because it is hard to make and costs a lot of money, as manufacturers typically believe. This is incompetence. Customers pay only for what is of use to them and gives them value. Nothing else constitutes quality. —Peter Drucker*

"Here's what I want you to do. You're going to write up what we just discussed as a business proposal and you're going to send it to a potential client. Keep it short and sweet. But be sure to *monetize the ROI*. Then wait for their response."

Well, that's exactly what he did. Being a great writer, he finished the homework I'd assigned him in two hours and had his polished proposal ready to send out. He then shot it off to a prospect via email. Four days later, he called me out of breath and ecstatic.

"You're not going to believe this!" he screamed. "I sent the proposal you told me to type up to a prospect. I did exactly like you told me, I broke down his ROI by monetizing how few units he'd need to sell to make back the investment in my services and BAM! He jumped right on it and signed up the very next day! The contract is for $34,000! And it only took me two hours to implement the strategy you gave me!"

"I'm proud of you," I told him. "But there's just one thing you did wrong."

He sat silently on the other end of the phone.

"You charged him WAY TOO LITTLE!" I teased. "He got one *heck* of a deal! He's not $34,000 in debt, he's about to be one RICH, RICH dude!" I chuckled.

The lesson: Monetize the ROI and the sale will take care of itself.

Go back and read this section over and over until it sinks in. When it does, you will be bounding down the Kangaroo Millionaire path and on your way toward massive riches and a peace of mind few will ever find.

Do what I'm telling you.

You won't be sorry.

Monetize the ROI.

TAKE ACTION NOW!

• Everything you say and do must be focused on the value it brings to others. Communicate in ways that neutralize perceived "debt" to show others how much they are going to profit from the way you rain value and service down upon your clients and customers.

• Adopt the entrepreneurial mindset that ROI is all that matters, because it is. Kangaroo Millionaires understand that wealth is a function of leveraging value. You have to think differently. ROI reigns supreme.

• Monetize the ROI. In your mind, in the prospects mind, in everyone's mind. Always, always, always monetize the ROI. Do that and you will make wise and transformational changes in your life and the lives of those whom you serve.

Obliterating the Start-Up Capital Excuse

Everywhere I go, in every city I travel when speaking, I encounter the same excuse-making from would-be entre-preneurs. Here's how it goes:

I have so many great ideas that I know could make mountains of money. But I don't have the seed money necessary to get my ideas off the ground. If only I had the start up money, I *know* I could make millions. But I barely have anything in savings, and now with the financial crisis, I'll probably *never* have enough capital to get my business started. I guess the old saying is true: it takes money to make money.

You know what? I'm so sick and tired of hearing the same tired, whiny, excuse script that I've decided to once and for all do something that I'm probably a fool for doing. Right now, right here, I'm going to SOLVE your small business startup capital problem. The information I'm about to give you may be worth millions to you. In fact, it's the exact same secret that I used when I was starting out that launched my entrepreneurial career—and that sent me bounding toward success.

Two words: credit cards.

Now, I know, I know, I know…we've been told all our lives that credit cards are evil. Your parents warned that you should never put things on them. You were told that Americans are maxed out on credit card debt. And guess what? This is true! Americans are up to their eyes with debt.

But here's what's also true: Credit cards can be one of the best ways for upstart entrepreneurs to secure the critical startup capital they need quickly. With access to credit loans growing increasingly tight, credit cards may very well end up being one of the only dependable and consistent means that average people can access the capital they need to create millionaire wealth.

"What the heck are you talking about?" you may be saying to yourself. "My credit limit is super low."

I don't doubt this. Do you know *why* your credit limit is low? I'll tell you. It's because YOU HAVEN'T CALLED AND HAD IT RAISED!

As shocking as it sounds, with a simple phone call you can have your credit limit raised significantly. Most people are surprised by how much they can increase their credit limit. And since most people have several credit cards, the combined effect after raising all your cards will be a serious chunk of change. I've seen people spend less than 20 minutes on the phone with their credit card companies and have raised over $100,000 in available capital to fund their upstart, as well as the educational and business-related tools they needed to start it. Typically, people with four or more cards walk away having raised between $10,000 to $25,000 of available funds. And all with a few phone calls. People never cease to be amazed at how simple it truly is.

"Yeah, yeah, yeah, I hear you," you may be saying to yourself, "but I don't want to incur massive interest payments and late fee penalties."

What if I told you there was a simple and smart way to never ever pay those exorbitant interest rates that most credit card companies charge? What would that do for your ability to get the education, training, and business tools you will need to help you reach your millionaire goal within the next 2-3 years? Obviously it would massively help you reach your goals. So let's do it! Let's raise the best kind of entrepreneurial dough on the planet, something called OPM (Other People's Money)!

TAKE ACTION NOW!

• Go raise your credit card capital. Heck, even if you don't use it, who cares? The exercise alone will teach you that the "startup capital excuse" is a bunch of hooey! Remember: millionaire is a mindset.

• Read Robert Kiyosaki's book, *Cashflow Quadrant*. Robert does a great job of teaching students the basic principles and importance of cashflow.

• Invest in your education about asset protection. What's the point of generating capital if you allow the government to rob you blind? Learn how to keep Uncle Sam's greedy fingers off your hard earned money.

HOW TO RAISE UP TO $50,000 AND BEYOND IN LESS THAN 20 MINUTES USING YOUR CREDIT CARDS... WITHOUT PAYING INTEREST OR FINANCE CHARGES EVER!!!

You know those checks your credit card company sends all the time? Yeah, well those are sheets of capital upstart gold. Using the strategy below you can float your cards and never pay interest or finances charges and thereby free up your monthly cash flow until you are ready to pay off the capital placed on your cards.

Credit card companies send you three types of checks:

• **Balance Transfer Checks:** These checks allow you to transfer a balance from a higher interest rate card to a lower interest rate card, typically at zero percent.

• **Convenience Checks:** These checks charge you a fee to use of typically between zero percent to four percent or a pre-set one-time fee, whichever is cheaper. If you have to use these checks that's fine; the cost to use them is generally cheaper than any other loan you would be able to use. So, for example, if you secured $35,000 x 4% fee that would equal $1,400 divided by 12 months for a cost of $116.66 per month. This amount will then be added to your monthly amount. So, if you float this amount for, say, two years, this is a 1,250% return on your monthly fees to access this money.

- **Courtesy Checks:** These typically charge you nothing to use. That's what you want! When you get those sheets of checks in the mail, Courtesy Checks are usually the first one or ones on the sheet, followed by the Convenience Checks.

After calling your credit cards and getting your limits raised as high as possible (this is as simple as a phone call, believe it or not), you're now ready to raise some capital for your business!

1. Charge the amount needed on credit card "A." Let's say it's $35,000.00.

2. Before card A's due date (5-9 days), write yourself a Courtesy Check from another card (card "B") for $35,000.00 and deposit it into your bank checking account.

3. After the deposit is made into your checking account, you will now write a check for $35,000.00 or have the $35,000.00 drafted out of your account to pay the total amount of the card off....not paying any interest or financing charges.

CHAPTER THREE

BE THE STUPIDEST PERSON IN THE ROOM

Why Being Smart Isn't

Brains are an asset…if you hide them. —Mae West

Everyone likes to feel smart.

Get over it!

Feeling stupid will make you much, much richer.

Why?

I'll tell you why: It's because surrounding yourself with smarter people is the smartest thing you'll ever do…even if it ends up making you feel like the stupidest person in the room, which, by definition, you will be.

Being an entrepreneur means burning your ego and focusing on what matters most—providing those you serve (a.k.a. your clients or customers) with superior service or products. And the only way you can do that is to realize what all Kangaroo Millionaires realize: Your success depends entirely on getting the right educational knowledge, the right mentors to help you steer your course, and the right team of bright and brilliant folks who can implement and execute your wealth-building strategies.

That's it. That's the secret. And notice that at every step of the process you will, by definition, be the stupidest person in the room.

> If your business depends on you, you don't own a business—you have a job. And it's the worst job in the world because you're working for a lunatic! And besides, that's not the purpose of going into business. The purpose of going into business is to get free of a job so you can create jobs for other people...So you can live an expanded, stimulating new life. —Michael Gerber, *The E-Myth Revisited*

It Ain't IQ

If IQ equaled riches, Albert Einstein would have been the world's richest man.

He wasn't.

If IQ equaled wealth, MENSA members would all be billionaires.

They aren't.

If raw, innate intelligence were a prerequisite for a fat bank account, I would never have enjoyed success in business.

As I've shared with you, I was your Average Joe student in high school. Fancy diplomas and expensive educations do not make high income earners.

I am absolutely convinced that any person of average intelligence, armed with the right education and Kangaroo mentoring their path, can become a millionaire within 2 to 3 years.

Hard work, focus, and a desire to overcome are what you need, not a big brain that fires synapses at Mach speed. Research on intelligence as a factor of income all points to the same conclusion: It ain't IQ! It's the desire to succeed, stupid!

> *Be wiser than other people if you can, but do not tell them so.* —Lord Chesterfield

These findings remind me of the story about the Yale University President some years ago who gave this advice to another university president.

"Always be kind to your A and B students. Someday one of them will return to your campus as a good teacher. And also be kind to your C students. Someday one of them will return and build your department a $10 million science laboratory."

It's not a mistake that so many millionaires and billionaires either dropped out of college or never bothered to go in the first place.

But you want to know my all-time favorite piece of proof that fancy and impressive degrees don't equate to financial freedom and a successful life?

Finance professors.

Now, if you're reading this and you ARE a finance professor, please know that I respect your commitment to education and higher learning. But the simple fact is that most finance professors don't make anywhere near a million dollars a year. Isn't this odd? Shouldn't people with PhD's in how financial markets rise, fall, and function have some kind of superior understanding of how to create and sustain wealth? And yet they don't, at least not in real terms. Most make a solid university salary. But they aren't all millionaires, despite their obvious intellectual and academic credentials.

Again, I'm not trying to be cute here. I really want you to marinate your mind on the powerful message embedded in that truth. Here you have people who have devoted their entire lives to the study of complex financial principles, market fluctuations, exchange rates, and global patterns of trade and commerce, and yet even *they* have not managed to find their way into the millionaires club. The reason isn't because they aren't smart enough; in terms of purely IQ, clearly they are among the best and brightest. No, the reason is that getting massively rich has almost nothing to do with a person's raw, innate intellectual talent.

So what *does* it have to do with? What is the single-most important attribute of seven-figure earners?

I will tell you.

It's follow-through, otherwise known as execution.

If you finish what you start, especially when adversity arises or challenges threaten to slow you down or crash your efforts, you have the tools needed to make millions. Follow-through is the spring in every Kangaroo Millionaire's step. You have to be willing to slog it out and triumph over adversity and setbacks. If you want it bad enough, success will come to you. It has nothing to do with IQ. It has everything to do with follow-through.

I think the fact that the road to riches has little to do with raw brain power is a blessing, actually. You know, sometimes we become so convinced of our own brilliance that we end up making ourselves look extremely silly and foolish. Sort of like the two taxidermists who stopped before a window in which an owl was on display. They immediately began to criticize the way it was mounted. Its eyes were not natural; its wings were not in proportion with its head; its feathers were not neatly arranged; and its feet could be improved.

When they had finished their criticism, the old owl turned his head—and winked at them.

TAKE ACTION NOW!

- Let go of the societal obsession with intelligence. Thank God that brainiacs exist…someone has to invent all these gadgets and toys that Kangaroo Millionaires buy with their massive riches!

- If you really want to build your "intelligence," focus on building your financial smarts by learning the high-percentage wealth strategies that give you the highest odds of achieving 7-figure status.

• If you need further proof that big brains don't always equal big bucks, just for kicks, go on Facebook and look up the valedictorian and salutatorian of your high school graduating class. Are they millionaires? Alright then. It ain't IQ. It's the drive and determination that will send you springing ahead in life and wealth.

• God gave you a beautiful brain filled with all you need to maximize your human potential. Be grateful for the mind God gave you. Then get busy putting it to good use by finding others with even bigger brains who can do what you can't!

Let Go of Ego & Hire All-Stars

Everyone has an ego. Even people who think of themselves as humble are, well, inflating their own sense of selflessness!

Regardless, no one likes to have their flaws pointed out and called to the attention of others. As Jacques Plante, a former professional goalie for the Montreal Canadians once said, "How would you like it in your job if every time you made a small mistake, a red light went on over your desk and fifteen thousand people stood up and yelled at you?"

He's got a point. I guess we should all be thankful that we don't have to endure that kind of public humiliation if and when we mess up. But the simple fact is that there are people out there who are far smarter and better at doing things that we're deficient in. Kangaroo Millionaires locate, hire, and hang on to the best talent they can find.

> *The first method for estimating the intelligence of a ruler is to look at the men he has around him. —Niccolo Machiavelli*

David Ogilvy (1911-1999) understood this core principle. Ogilvy built one of the world's greatest advertising agencies during his lifetime. In addition to being a wonderfully creative person, he was also a great administrator and business builder.

In his book, *Ogilvy on Advertising*, Ogilvy tells how, when someone was appointed to head one of Ogilvy and Mather's growing number of offices, he would send as a gift a Russian nesting doll. Inside the smallest doll, he placed this note: "If each of us hires people who are smaller than we are, we shall become a company of dwarfs. But if each of us hires people who are bigger than we are, we shall become a company of giants."

That's a philosophy I have always followed in my entrepreneurial ventures and one I encourage you to adopt as well. When assembling my team, I go out and find the best and brightest. If I interview someone who knows less than me I don't hire them. Superior people create superior solutions. And that's what I want.

TAKE ACTION NOW!

- If you think you are the center of the universe, you're in the wrong galaxy. Humility is the beginning of true confidence and leadership. Swagger and success aren't synonymous. Hire smart folks.

• Read the obituaries. Doing so will remind you that each day is a blessing.

• Live accordingly.

• When you feel yourself becoming prideful or pompous, volunteer at a homeless shelter or similar organizations. Learn the art of cutting yourself down to size so that others or circumstances won't do it for you.

• Take a 3x5 card each morning and dash off a statement of gratitude and tape it above your computer monitor. It can be serious or silly, but try it and see what happens. Save all the cards in a box in your desk drawer. Then, each month, sift through your "30 or 31 Days of Gratitude." This exercise is more powerful than you can imagine. Try it. Grab a card and jot down your gratitude statement NOW.

Run Toward Problems, Not Away From Them

In 1879, Procter and Gamble's best seller was candles. But the company was in trouble. Thomas Edison had invented the light bulb, and it looked as if candles would become obsolete. Their fears became reality when the market for candles

> *Humility is always one play away.*
> —Tom Foley, *Miami Dolphins*

plummeted since customers now only bought them for use on special occasions.

The outlook appeared to be bleak for Procter and Gamble. However, at this time, it seemed that destiny played a dramatic part in pulling the struggling company from the clutches of bankruptcy. A forgetful employee at a small factory in Cincinnati forgot to turn off his machine when he went to lunch. The result? A frothing mass of lather filled with air bubbles.

He almost threw the stuff away but instead decided to make it into soap. The soap floated. Thus, Ivory soap was born and became the mainstay of the Procter and Gamble Company.

Why was the soap that floats such a hot item at that time? In Cincinnati, during that period, some people bathed in the Ohio River. Floating soap didn't sink and consequently never got lost. So, Ivory soap became a best seller in Ohio and eventually across the country.

Like Procter and Gamble, Kangaroo Millionaires never give up when things go wrong or when seemingly insurmountable problems arise. Creativity can change a problem and turn it into a goldmine.

But there's another sense in which you should always run toward—not away from—problems. And that deals with your ability to identify and neutralize problems as they arise. Business owners who communicate to their employees that problems are catastrophic and to be avoided at all costs end up doing far more harm than good.

> *Customers who complain are your friends because they are giving you a chance to improve instead of just walking away. —Stew Leonard*

You must create a climate in which those you work with feel comfortable coming to you as problems arise. They need to feel that you will not "shoot the messenger" but will instead support them for bringing potential pitfalls to your attention promptly. Problems are just opportunities in disguise. Furthermore, you can't solve what you can't sense. And if you don't see a problem you can't fix it.

Henry Ford understood the importance of addressing problems. The auto pioneer was once asked why he made a habit of visiting his executives when problems arose, rather than inviting them to his own office.

"I go to them to save time," Ford explained, "and besides… I've found I can leave their office a lot quicker than I can get them to leave mine."

TAKE ACTION NOW!

- Go create a FREE survey on Survey Monkey (www.surveymonkey.com) that analyzes your organization's present weaknesses. Then distribute it to your business associates. You can't fix what you don't identify. If you're REALLY bold, create a survey form analyzing your own leadership weaknesses and let your friends, family members, or colleagues fill it out anonymously and with an assurance that there will be no hurt feelings or retributions. The feedback you gather may transform your life and business.

• Invite your employees and associates to share the problems they've noticed. Don't allow them to candy coat conditions. That's putting problems on a layaway plan. Encourage constructive, solution-focused critical feedback.

• When you identify a weak link, find a real solution. Band-aid solutions breed infections that fester and cause organizational illness. If you aren't good with numbers, outsource the bean counting to someone who is. If your eyes glaze over when it comes to writing reports or white papers, hire a copywriter who loves the stuff. But whatever you do, don't shrink from weaknesses, run toward them.

• Create a system for gathering critical feedback. Make others feel safe to offer constructive criticism.

Undersell Your Skills & Exhibit Confident Humility

In the office of the late Alex Haley, author of *Roots*, hung a picture of a turtle sitting on a fence. When Haley looked at it, he would be reminded of a lesson taught to him by his friend John Gaines: "If you see a turtle on top of a fence post, you know he had some help."

Said Haley, "Any time I start thinking, 'Wow, isn't this marvelous what I've done!' I look at that picture and remember how this turtle—me—got up on that post."

> *A sense of humor…is the ability to understand a joke—*
> *and that the joke is oneself.* —Clifton Fadiman

Kangaroo Millionaires develop a powerful sense of confidence. Yet they also realize that true inner confidence doesn't have to have a flashing neon sign above it that screams, "I'm confident! I'm confident! I promise…I'm really, really confident!"

No, instead, Kangaroo Millionaires downplay their importance and in the process elevate their perceived power and command.

You know this in your own life. For example, that guy at the gym where you work out who everyone knows is the strongest, baddest, toughest dude in the whole joint. You know the one. The guy who can bench press more plates than there is room on the bar. Yeah, that guy. Well, I bet that guy is wearing a floppy t-shirt, some ragged shorts, and probably doesn't even wear weight training gloves. You know why? He doesn't have to show off because everyone in the place knows he's strong. He doesn't feel the need to showboat. There's no reason to. In fact, if he did, he would seem weaker, not stronger.

The same is true for you. If you want to attract high-quality, highly talented individuals, there's no need to come across as arrogant or self-important. People can sense power. It fills the room. It announces itself quietly and definitively. Better still, it attracts others to it and doesn't repel people from it.

That reminds me of the story about the self-important chief executive officer who arrived at the hotel ballroom where his company's annual meeting was to be held and was stopped at the door by a uniformed guard.

The guard was about six-foot-five and weighed at least 250 pounds.

"Just wait here," said the guard, "until I check."

"But," sputtered the CEO, "don't you know who I am?"

"No, sir," said the guard, "but I will go and find out and let you know."

TAKE ACTION NOW!

• Let others find out what a big deal you are on their own. Nothing impresses someone like someone who seems unimpressed by themselves.

• Don't show your hand right away. Hold some of your biggest cards close to the vest.

• Ask questions. Tons and tons of questions. The thing people love to talk about more than anything else is themselves. Let them. They'll love you for it.

• The hard sell (of yourself or your company) turns people off. Use stories and testimonials to showcase your skills and talents. Stories don't raise the red flag of the hard sell. They sound natural and free flowing—all while allowing you to share the amazing things you or your company have done and can do for others. Use stories and client testimonials to sell yourself.

Incentivize Excellence

Anyone who has been around business speakers or seminars has at some point heard the phrase "Reward Excellence."

I disagree.

You don't just want to reward excellence. You want to incentivize it!

Your high performers are the ones who matter most. They are the engines of your entrepreneurial vessel.

Take great care of them!

Keep them happy!

Make sure to do as David Kim, the CEO of Baja Fresh, likes to say and "slap a pair of happiness handcuffs on them!"

Look, the so-called "war for talent" that business leaders and magazines always talk about is real. The simple fact is finding the best people will be difficult—*extremely* hard. And it's only going to get harder. How come? Well, much of the reason has to do with demographics. As business writer Charles Fishman, writing for *Fast Company* magazine notes:

In 15 years, there will be 15% fewer Americans in the 35- to 45-year-old range than there are now. At the same time, the U.S. economy is likely to grow at a rate of 3% to 4% per year. So over that period, the demand for bright, talented 35- to 45-year olds will increase by, say, 25%, and the supply will be going down by 15%. That sets the stage for a talent war.[11]

When you find someone who is truly exceptional and a rare talent, incentivize their performance by giving them a percentage of the action. High achievers like a challenge. Set goals and let them soar high enough to reach them. And when they do, reward them handsomely.

The reason for this should be obvious: high achievers have tons of options. They can pick up and leave at any moment. And then where will you be? You'll be out scrounging around trying to find someone who can keep pace and who has a fraction of the talent as the star you had but let get away.

Don't do that.

Remember: You should *want* to be the "stupidest" person in the room. That means finding the smarties and holding on to them for dear life.

Some newbie entrepreneurs think that there is a limitless pool of talent out there. But talk to any hiring personnel director and they will tell you otherwise. Sure, there's a lot of good out there, but great? Not so much. Outstanding? Even fewer.

Don't be unwise in how you handle your all-stars.

Keep them happy and they will return the favor.

TAKE ACTION NOW!

- If you've never taken an IQ test, don't. It's unimportant and has zero to do with how high you can climb. Anyone of average intelligence can become a millionaire. If you doubt this, my high school teachers will be happy to confirm this to be true. Kangaroo Millionaires need not be geniuses, but they sure as heck don't mind hiring them.

• Know who your high flyers are and keep them close. Find out what they want and give it to them.

• Realize that it's far easier to keep a star than it is to have to go out and search for, attract, and train another one. Keep your hotshots happy and feeling appreciated. It's not only polite, it's profitable.

CHAPTER FOUR

BE LAZY

The Worker Bee Is Still a Worker.
Be the Queen

Riches, when they come in huge quantities, are never the result of HARD work! Riches come, if they come at all, in response to definite demands, based upon the application of definite principles, and not by chance or luck. —Napoleon Hill, *Author of Think and Grow Rich*

Famous funny man Will Rogers once asked President Calvin Coolidge how he kept fit in a job that had broken the health and the spirit of his predecessor, Woodrow Wilson.

"By avoiding the big problems," the President answered seriously.

Coolidge wasn't kidding. He worked only four hours of a day and took a nap every afternoon.

Good work if you can get it.

Oh, by the way—you can.

You may not be able to get away with four-hour workdays all the time, despite what Timothy Ferris might tell you in his great and bestselling book *The Four-Hour Work Week*, but the point is well-taken.

Even the most powerful man in the world knew that the secret to success wasn't working himself to death, but rather understanding his strengths, delegating to others the tasks that were best done by someone else, and focusing his energy on the important decisions he needed to make.

Here are six ways to be "lazy"—and still accomplish everything you need to do without running yourself into the ground.

Do-It-Yourself Is D-U-M-B

The movie *Funny Farm* is an oldie but a goodie.

Chevy Chase plays a writer who moves away from New York City with his lovely, very proper wife for a New England paradise, where he plans to fix up their house, write a novel, and start a family.

You can imagine what happens.

The king of slapstick makes a mess of the place and instead of fixing it, he only makes it worse. His wife discovers a body buried in the garden. The book that he was supposed to write never gets written. And his lovely wife leaves him.

It's only when the two enlist the help of the locals—the people who can get things done—that they reunite and everybody lives happily ever after.

Sure, it's only a movie.

But there's a lot of truth to the notion that you hire the people who know how to get things done: plumbers plumb, architects build, electricians run wire.

When it comes to do-it-yourself, you probably think a whole lot like I used to think. If you want something done right, you do it yourself.

> *Hire people who are better than you are, then leave them to get on with it. Look for people who will aim for the remarkable, who will not settle for the routine. — David Ogilvy*

Maybe that was true once, when you couldn't be sure where to find reliable help or you didn't know how you were going to pay for it. But these days, the secret to getting things done is knowing *how* to get things done—and taking advantage of all the information you have at your fingertips.

Remember, doing it yourself is, well, just plain dumb!

If your time isn't worth more than grunt work then you're doing something wrong. Dollarize your time by calculating how much money you can generate per hour and then use this as a benchmark for determining what you can outsource.

Once you make a decision, trust it. You wouldn't be reading this book if you were a bad judge of character and couldn't trust your own instincts.

Now, sit back and count all the time and money you're saving by not doing it yourself.

TAKE ACTION NOW!

• Identify the areas that are draining your time—the things that someone else could do for you.

• Create a budget for outsourcing. If the word "budget" sends shivers up your spine, start out by getting your financial house in organized and in order. Go grab your FREE money management, budget, planning, and financial planning software at Mint (www.mint.com).

• Go online. Network. Get yourself plugged in to the people and the places that will help you to make the most of your time.

• Resist the temptation to slip back into a DIY mindset.

"Crises" Seldom Are

In my first days as a firefighter, I learned in a hurry the difference between a crisis and the things that weren't important enough to sweat. Rushing to the scene of an accident or struggling to save a family from a burning house as they watch their possessions go up in flames tends to put things in perspective. You quickly learn what's important and what's not.

A good rule of thumb might be Abraham Lincoln's response to the possibility that America was going to be split in two during his administration. When asked what his policy was going to be, Lincoln replied, "I have none. I pass my life in preventing the storm from blowing down the tent, and I drive in the pegs as fast as they are pulled."

Sometimes, life doesn't give us clear-cut examples.

You know, the little things that get in your way in the course of a day.

The things you want to take care of but don't have the time for.

The things you don't like to do.

A real crisis is one where you can feel the tent pegs starting to loosen and the world come apart around you.

It happens, but not as often as you think. Springing toward wealth will require you to tell the difference between the mundane and the must-respond. Trust me, this is one of the most important skills any entrepreneur can develop.

The tough survive. You will face crisis, and you will handle it well. Keep your powder dry and ready to fire when it really needs to be used.

> *When written in Chinese, the word "crisis" is composed of two characters—one represents danger and one represents opportunity.* —John F. Kennedy

But in your own business, on the vast majority of days that don't require you to go into full crisis mode, you need to stop sweating the small stuff—and realize that most of it is, as the saying goes, "the small stuff."

I'm not suggesting that you follow the mantra in the old Seinfeld episode—"serenity now"—and let everything work itself out. But knowing what's important and being able to prioritize are vital to the smooth and efficient operation of any business.

For the day-to-day stuff, learn to train others by ignoring time-wasting activities that rob you of productivity and plunk you deep into informational quicksand. After all, when was the last time you saw a kangaroo trapped in a sinkhole?

Learn to hop over the parts of the day that drain your time.

For example, that friend who is constantly flooding your inbox with spam and stupid forwards...yeah, that friend. Well, send all his e-mails to a folder labeled "Junk to Ignore."

Or, better still, write them back and tell them that all their forwards are clogging up your digital pipes and that it's time to turn off the forwarding faucet.

Here's another tip: Get in the habit of "bundling" your e-mails by not clicking on every e-mail that dings throughout your day. Shut the dinger off and only check e-mail three times a day. The process of "bundling" saves tons of time and reduces distractions that rob you of getting things done.

Another thing that you need to keep in mind—an idea recommended by productivity pro and bestselling author Laura Stack—is that you should always "Do first what's due first." Don't put off doing something that you need to do (that is, anything that can't be done by someone else) when the only way to finish is to get your butt in the seat and start working.[12]

Procrastination doesn't mean being lazy, it means that you're avoiding the work that you need to do.

Learn to see your work for what it is—the quickest and surest way for you to realize your dream.

You'll be surprised how quickly things get done when you get in the habit of knocking out the stuff that's got to be done.

In that case, you're not working hard, just smart. And when you learn the difference between a crisis and a routine, you'll be on your way to freeing your time for other things. BE LAZY!

TAKE ACTION NOW!

- Learn to tell the difference between a crisis and a nuisance.

- Identify potential crises and put in place a contingency plan. Good planning lessens the potential for disaster.

- Internet marketing expert Eben Pagan, creator of the popular Wake Up Productive home study course, recommends setting a timer for 90 minutes and placing it on your desk. Refuse to get up from your chair and stop working before the timer dings. This is a powerful tip that can produce amazing results. Try it today.

• Have a "safe zone" where people can't get in touch with you. Maybe it's a home office, your car, the coffee shop down the street, even the lounge chair by your swimming pool. This ensures that you'll be able to work uninterrupted—a necessity if you want to handle routine tasks that can't be delegated to others.

• Break the work up into manageable chunks and start plowing away.

Hate Doing the Things You Hate

The more Richard Branson tried to compensate for his dyslexia as a child growing up in Britain, the more frustrated he got with his studies. Richard was popular with people and made friends easily, but he was hesitant to speak in public for fear that his condition might be discovered. You can't blame him for shying away from those situations.

His headmaster at his British boarding school, both concerned about Richard's progress and aware of the other extraordinary gifts that he possessed, wrote, "Branson, I predict that you will either go to prison or become a millionaire."[13]

How did that work out for him?

At age 20, he was operating a mail-order record business out of the trunk of his car. He called the enterprise Virgin, and the name has stuck through all of Richard's many ventures.

Seven years later, he signed the legendary punk-rock band the Sex Pistols to his own record label.

Seven years after that, he poked the world's largest airlines in the eye by founding Virgin Atlantic Airways.

And in 2007, he took on the world's largest telecommunication companies with the introduction of Virgin Media.

Now, of course, Richard is a multi-billionaire, one of the wealthiest entrepreneurs in the world, mastermind of 150 companies that carry the Virgin brand, and someone famous for his ability to connect with people on their level and to turn big ideas into big money.[14]

Would he have accomplished all of this if he had single-mindedly focused on things that he didn't enjoy, just because those around him thought he should?

Doubtful.

We all have things that we hate to do. We encounter them every day, but as a successful person, you learn to focus your strengths and the things you enjoy and to avoid doing the things you hate. Remember: laziness is a virtue!

> *The surest way for an executive to kill himself*
> *is to refuse to learn how, and when,*
> *and to whom to delegate work.* — J. C. Penney

Right now I want you to write down the top three things you dread most about your business.

Is it HTML programming?

Copywriting?

Graphic design?

Writing handwritten thank you notes?

Scheduling?

Keeping up with your social networking sites?

Booking travel?

Organizing your files?

Whatever it is, write it down. Now, guess what? Every single one of the items I've listed can be outsourced with the click of a mouse with the help of a personal outsourcing website and a virtual secretary.

Here are the top 5 sites you can visit right now:

- www.elance.com
- www.guru.com
- www.rentacoder.com
- www.craigslist.com
- www.iFreelance.com

Best of all, posting a project or job on these sites is FREE!

Heck, what do you have to lose?

See how much it would cost to have someone handle the junk you dread. Then refer back to your dollarized hour and determine whether it makes sense to drop the dough and outsource the headaches you hate.

TAKE ACTION NOW!

- Refuse to do the things you hate to do.

- Right now, go list three outsourcing jobs at one of the Web sites listed above. Stop reading this sentence and go list them already. It's FREE!

- Calculate your cost savings from outsourcing the things you HATE to do!

- Find and hire people who *love* to do the things you hate.

Scarcity = Value (Or, Learning to Make Yourself Scarce)

U.S. Army Sergeant Brendan Kitchens worked "outside the wire" every day on patrol in Kandahar, Afghanistan, putting his life on the line to protect our freedom.

But when he found out in 2004 that he was one of only ten service members in the world who would get to talk to the President of the United States during the traditional Thanksgiving phone calls, Sergeant Kitchens jumped at the chance.

"It's a once in a lifetime opportunity," Kitchens said. "This'll be something to tell my kids and something to tell people about for the rest of my life."[15]

When the President of the United States calls you, he doesn't do so directly. Instead, he has the White House operators call you first, gets you on the phone, confirms that you are the person whom he wishes to speak with, and then says, "Hold please for the President of the United States." Now, think about it. Why all those extra layers of protocol and protection?

Because powerful people are hard to reach.

But there you sit, feeling the invisible power surging through the phone as you wait in anxious anticipation. By the time the President picks up the line on his end, you're grateful that he still remembers you're there.

Most of us will never get a phone call from the President, so let me give you another example of the scarcity principle we can all relate to: dating.

In an article titled, "Want to be wanted? Make yourself scarce," Fred Gonzalez relates the story of a friend who met a guy on Match.com. After a couple of nice dates, the guy disappeared.

"For a couple of weeks [he] vanished from the radar," Gonzalez writes. "She was bummed and wondered if perhaps he didn't like her. I suggested she wait, that he may really be busy (and employing the rule). Regardless, he was on her mind as someone who seemed unattainable. He finally did email back, much to her excitement, and they have planned another date."[16]

In business, distance equals scarcity. And scarcity makes you appear busy, important, and powerful. Ironically, if your customers have direct access to you, your perceived stature and importance will nosedive. You have to learn the methods of millionaires. Read this paragraph again and let it really sink in. This principle will make you rich.

Go look out your window. Do you see a kangaroo? Probably not. Kangaroos are often hard to find. You should be too. I know that may seem counterintuitive, but that's precisely why it works and will help you build wealth.

Think about celebrities and VIPs. Can you just walk straight up to them? Usually not. Typically they are surrounded by a ring of handlers, schedulers, publicists, hair and makeup stylists, their agent, and other members of their entourage.

If you approach your favorite movie star in a restaurant, be prepared to get tackled by some hulking bodyguard with bulging muscles—a dude who gets paid well to keep people like you away from their clients. The result of these layers of separation is that it makes people want to be on the INSIDE of their circle all the more!

There's a downside to celebrity, of course, and every famous person wakes up in cold sweats at night thinking about it: OVEREXPOSURE. When the supply exceeds demand, you've got a big problem. Here again, we prove the golden principle: Scarcity reigns supreme.

Why is gold valuable? Why are diamonds valuable? Why is anything valuable? Because *you* give it value.

Take the example of James Bond in the movie *Diamonds Are Forever*.

In it, Bond—Sean Connery at his best—spends a lot of time trying to track down his old nemesis, Ernst Blofeld, who's always trying to blow up the world.

But—stick with me here—the really interesting character is a guy called Willard Whyte, a reclusive billionaire who apparently spends most of his life in the penthouse of a Las Vegas casino (he's patterned after American tycoon Howard Hughes, one of the most reclusive, eccentric—*and sought after*—men on the planet during the height of his powers in the 1960s).

What's the result of Whyte's scarcity? I'll tell you. The appearance that he's not within reach. HE'S IN DEMAND!

Heck, Bond has to rappel the side of the casino just to try to get a glimpse of him.

Doesn't sound like a half-bad idea, huh, keeping yourself hidden away from the world while people clamor to get a piece of you? Seeing only the people that you want and need to see—and increasing your desirability in the process.

Making yourself scarce isn't as difficult as you think it is.

It means hiring an assistant who handles your scheduling, fields your calls, even calls your clients and has them wait on the line for you to be patched through on the call. These details matter more than you realize. They create a zone of power and authority.

They also send a message to your clients that your time is VALUABLE. It trains them not to waste your time but to respect it.

> *The Scarcity Rule is kind of like knowing the perfect time to leave the house party or dinner party on a high note so as to not overextend your stay.* — Fred Gonzalez

Even if you work out of your home office, hire a Virtual Assistant. Be sure to get one who knows what she or he is doing, has stellar writing skills (for e-mail, typing, and other correspondence) and a pleasant and professional voice when calling on your behalf. In addition to my regular staff, I have a virtual assistant. She gives me 45 hours a month, and I don't have to pay for equipment and employment taxes or worry about vacation and sick leave. She's the best, and her rates are very reasonable (check out her company's services and tell her Marc sent you: www.my-personal-secretary.com, especially given how good she is at what she does. But prices and fees vary among virtual assistants.

Remember: The people you surround yourself with are an extension of you. They leave an impression about you whether you want them to or not. So make sure they speak grammatically correct sentences and sound warm, intelligent, and professional.

You want to cultivate an image of being "super busy" so that when people DO get a piece of your time they get excited and refuse to waste the opportunity you've afforded them. But again, you have to train your clients and associates. People who are glad to be with you are willing to do more for you than those who expect you to be at their beck and call.

TAKE ACTION NOW!

- Learn to make yourself scarce.

- When dealing with important clients, never call them directly. Create distance by first having your assistant call your clients and put them on hold.

• When a new client contacts you via e-mail, have your assistant respond with a message that conveys how busy you are.

• Cultivate your perceived scarcity—visually, online, and with all your public relations. Train others not to waste or devalue your time.

No Dough, No Go

Humorist Erma Bombeck had it right when she said, "House guests should be regarded as perishable: Leave them out too long, and they go bad."

You've been a victim of the guests who just won't leave. You know, Clark Griswold's Cousin Eddie and his family, who show up for Christmas in an old RV and intend to stay for a month. It doesn't help that Eddie hasn't had a job in seven years. Clark takes the visit with his usual good humor, but everyone has his limits. Moments of hilarity ensue, much of it based on the fact that Eddie is a deadbeat.

Yeah, you know them.

You enjoy their company for a while, even if they are a little eccentric. But they won't take a hint. After two weeks, several increasingly stern invitations to leave, and a lot of hurt feelings, they're still on the couch, smearing Cheetos dust on the cushions, watching reality shows, harassing the dog, and wondering why you don't want to spend more time with them or if you'll give them a ride to the mall later.

Or maybe you've had the roommate from hell, the guy or gal who never paid their share of the food or the utilities, yet threw a great party every weekend with the money they saved from not chipping in on the necessities.

Or the acquaintance you run into on the street, the one who never quite realizes why you keep sneaking not-so-subtle glances at your watch to let him know that you've got someplace to be.

Unfortunately, a lot of clients are like that, too. When they pay—*if* they pay—they don't pay you what you're worth. They don't respect the value of your service and your time.

In 2005, American businesses recorded non-payments of $180 billion. Nearly half of all small businesses complained of payments slow in coming.[17]

> *Until you value yourself, you won't value your time. Until you value your time, you won't do anything with it.* —M. Scott Peck

No matter where you are in your career, you have to have this mindset: *Of all the businesses out there, your business is the one that can least afford to serve clients who are dragging down your bottom line.*

That's not selfish, it's practical.

In her article "Fire Your Bad Clients," Pam Newman lists the five different kinds of clients to avoid: focus drainers, low-profitability clients, complainers, "something for nothing" clients, and time wasters.[18]

Some clients can fit into more than one category. Those are the no-brainers, the ones you need to fire immediately. Others may fall into a gray area, and you may be hesitant to fire clients who could turn out to be good business partners one day.

While it's generally a good idea to trust your gut when making those sorts of decisions, you need to take a good, hard look at the pros and cons of keeping deadbeat clients on your roll.

Forewarned is forearmed. Fire them now, before you regret your inaction.

One of the main reasons businesses won't fire clients is a misguided sense of loyalty. We all want others to succeed—after all, the more other businesses succeed, the more likely they'll be able to afford your services.

But enough is enough.

In a *Wall Street Journal* blog, Wendy Bounds calls it the "'dollar bill' syndrome," the inability for so many of us to fire clients—even when they really deserve it.

"Walk into small businesses across the country and you'll frequently see a crumpled dollar bill framed on the wall as proof of the first sale that company ever made. . . . Because, let's face it, when you're starting out, there's always a bit of will-they-come fear lurking in the belly. Which is why so many entrepreneurs have a hard time cutting off clients who fall behind with payments."[19]

A friend of mind puts it another way, one less kind: "Undeserved loyalty gets more people in trouble than the crime itself." The point is, you need to know when to stop worrying about your clients and start worrying about yourself. Know when to cut your losses.

Stop wasting your time on clients or activities that don't fatten your wallet. Every single year you need to "fire" your bottom 10% of clients. They are cutting into your profit margins and holding you back from climbing higher.

It's a truism in business—you don't just represent your clients, your clients represent you. They're the face of your company when they talk to their friends—or other prospective clients.

Who do you want coming to you, the client who's going to make you look good by paying you what you're worth and taking your relationship to the next level? Or the client who's going to try to nickel-and-dime you until you finally work up the courage to fire them?

If you don't establish a pricing "floor" under which you refuse to go for new accounts or business deals, then you are limiting your ability to raise your profit ceiling. Is all this harsh? No, it's smart.

Let me put it this way: *Going higher means learning to fire.*

So drop your low-dollar accounts and your slow-payers. Now.

No, I mean right this second.

Dog-ear this page and then go e-mail your time-waster clients a polite, yet direct, message. Tell them that, due to overwhelming demand from your new client acquisitions and inquiries, you have been forced only to accept high-dollar accounts.

You don't have to like it, but you do need to do it. Your business depends on it.

From now on, stick hard and firm to a minimum amount that you'll take for your services.

TAKE ACTION NOW!

- Not all clients are created equal. Understand that underperforming clients drag you down.

- Fire the bottom 10% of your clients—including late payers. Now.

- Raise your fees. Most entrepreneurs underestimate the value of the work they do for their clients. If you don't know how much you should increase your fee by, double your current rates and just see what happens. You don't think this will work, but if you provide stellar service and value, it will. You will be amazed.

- Raise the bar on your target clientele. Choose your clients based on what they can do for *you*. Affluent clients are less sensitive to market downturns and high prices. Go for the gold.

Luxuriate Your Daily Lifestyle

So you were a little envious when you heard that Tiger Woods bought a 155-foot, $22 million yacht—appropriately called *Privacy*—so that he and his supermodel wife, Ellen, could go tooling around the world's oceans when he wasn't winning golf tournaments.

Who wasn't?

You know, I used to look at stories like that and wish like crazy I was the one standing beside the yacht, or playing golf on the championship course, or driving the expensive sports car.

And then I got to the point where I could do those things, and I realized something else. When you reach a certain level, after years and years of hard work, you need to make time for yourself.

No one else is going to do it for you.

Kind of like the old saying, "Sometimes you tread water for so long, you can't do anything else."

The point? Successful people are so driven by their vision and so busy making sure that they're always jumping ahead that sometimes they don't even bother to take care of their own needs.

It's the easiest thing in the world to just keep on working. You know, the Law of Inertia. Unless you're acted upon by some outside force that tells you that you need to treat yourself, you're going to keep on doing what you've been doing to get where you are.

Well, YOU are that outside force. Tell yourself that it's OK to luxuriate your everyday life.

Heck, it's not just OK. You *have* to do it.

Relaxation leads to a sound mind and a sound body—both of which you'll need for the long haul.

You know what? I take full advantage of the finer things every day, because I've learned that growing wealth means that you need to recharge your batteries.

Nobody works 24/7. Why would you want to?

Pamper yourself. Do the things you've always wanted to do. Take care of yourself first, and the rest will follow.

> *We are closer to the ants than to the butterflies. Very few people can endure much leisure. —Gerald Brenan*

It's a little counterintuitive, I know. After all, you've been taught all your life that you need to be frugal about everything you do. I was taught the same thing: Work hard, keep your head down, and 30 years later get a handshake and a gold watch.

And if you want to live a middle-class lifestyle and save a few bucks so that, when you retire after spending your entire adult life in the same job, you can take a vacation to the Grand Canyon...well then, quite honestly, I find your lack of vision and ambition depressing.

But what I'm talking about here is *really* taking care of yourself. Mind and body. So that you're ready to handle the big decisions and to take care of business when the time comes. You have to own your wealth, not the other way around.

I call it being the Queen Bee, taking care of your own enjoyment.

The queen just sits around the hive all day and has the drones do the work. Success breeds success (in the queen's case, literally).

You can do this in simple ways.

For example, do you like massages? Who doesn't?! Well, hop online and buy yourself a personal masseuse in the form of a Homedics Shiatsu back massager for about $125 and plop it into your favorite cushy chair at home. Then, when it's time to sort mail, edit documents, or read over a business report, flick on your massager and let the stress melt away while you work.

The number of similar items available is growing, and they're all reasonably priced—chairs with built-in MP3 players, ergonomic furniture, sound systems and online services that allow you to listen to any kind of music you could ever want.

You don't need to be a fan of feng shui to enjoy the spaces that you make for yourself at home (www.overstock.com).

You'll feel better, be more relaxed, and break the stress that holds your muscles in a vice grip.

That's just one example. Do you like a spa experience? Who doesn't?! So buy a portable spa machine to go in your bathtub and turn the mundane shower into a spa (www.homedics. com).

Read a book (www.bookcloseouts.com)

Go to dinner at a nice restaurant near your home (www. zagat.com)

Take time out for the important people in your life—take them on a vacation. Did you know you can go on an incredible vacation for peanuts? It's true. Check out www.gate1travel. com. Did you know that you can go on an incredible European vacation for less than a grand? Heck, sometimes less than $750? And that's everything included! Go check out the site and see what I'm talking about.

Plan and organize your virtual office with FREE software from ThinkFree Office (www.thinkfree.com).

The point of all this? Being the Queen Bee means finding ways to transform your daily life into a playground of pleasure and enjoyment.

TAKE ACTION NOW!

Believe that you deserve every luxury you give yourself. Relaxation is as much a part of success as the hard work you do to realize your dream.

Right now, take time to luxuriate your lifestyle—buy a subscription to a magazine you like, play a round of golf, buy tickets to your favorite sporting event.

Envision your future. Right now, set your screensaver to an image that represents your biggest dream—a secluded beach, a mountaintop in Europe, a luxury vehicle, even Tiger Woods' yacht.

Take good care of your employees. They'll return the favor many times over.

CHAPTER FIVE

PAY HIGH PRICES

Half-Price Gets You Half the Results

I do not prize the word "cheap." It is not a badge of honor. It is a symbol of despair. Cheap prices make for cheap goods; cheap goods make for cheap men; and cheap men make for a cheap country. —President William McKinley

As a kid, I had a friend, we'll call him "Steven," whose parents were always arguing about money. They never had enough and when we would go upstairs to play with Steven's toy soldiers or look at baseball cards, we could hear his parents arguing through the heating duct.

Steven's dad worked at a brick factory across town. It was a hard job. He didn't make nearly the money he should have for the amount of work he did. And he took every opportunity to scold Steven's mom for spending too much on various household items, even the basics.

The toilet paper was too plush, the name brand meats were too expensive, the pillow cases and sheets were too fine.

I didn't realize until much later that Steven's dad just had it wrong. By trying to get his wife to save money by buying inferior products, he had instead forced her to spend more money than if she had just gotten the higher-quality products in the first place.

Cheap toilet paper doesn't make anybody happy, and you use more of it. Cheap meat isn't good for you and doesn't taste right. Cheap sheets and pillow cases wear out too quickly and chaff your face when you're trying to get a good night's sleep.

It's only human nature to think the way Steven's dad did.

Here's the cold, hard truth: *half-price gets you half the results.*

Expertise is Priceless

You've heard the warnings:

Don't be pennywise and pound foolish.

You get what you pay for.

Don't sweat the small stuff and then leave the important things up to chance.

Well, sometimes the things we hear as kids actually make sense when we rethink them as adults. Truth is, when you pay attention to the details at the expense of the big picture, it's going to cost you and your business money.

The good news: The great wave in Internet commerce lately has been outsourcing. If you go to any of a number of sites that advertise copywriting or marketing or ghostwriting or phone and message service—just about anything you could ever want, really—you'll find a stunning range of estimates on what your job might cost.

And if you think you have a problem that can't be solved by outsourcing, consider this: When you google the term "outsourcing," you get back almost 52,800,000 hits!

One recent example among many is that of Tess Luu, who owns a furniture showroom in Las Vegas. When she decided to cut her overhead and move her business online, operating the business through outsourcers, she cut her operating costs by 75%.

"I would be bankrupt now had I not changed my model," Luu says.[20]

So you think you're in a business where outsourcing can't help?

> *A man takes his car into the shop to check out a rattling noise. The repairman looked under the hood, confidently picked up a rubber mallet, and started banging on the right side of the engine block. When he told the car owner to start the car—no more noise! Satisfied that the problem was solved, the owner went to the cashier to pay the bill and was stunned to see that he owed $107 dollars. When he confronted the mechanic, the man explained, "I charged you $7 for pounding on the engine with the rubber mallet and $100 for knowing where to pound, how hard to pound, and when to stop pounding."*

Ben Trowbridge, founder and CEO of Alsbridge, a Dallas consulting company that advises clients on outsourcing, says that every company, regardless of size—from a one-person operation to the Fortune 500—has the same problems when it comes to finding outsourcing help.

"It's classic for small businesses to outsource in waves," Trowbridge says. "Because the current financial crisis is acting as a catalyst for companies to seriously consider outsourcing, we are riding that wave."

After her decision to outsource, Luu has come to understand the importance of hiring the right people for the job.

"I wasted tens of thousands not hiring the right company for my programming and data entry," she says. "I ended up having to redo the work and spend time researching other firms and getting referrals before I found the right people."[21]

What Tess Luu discovered isn't unusual. Outsourcing efficiently is like any other skill—it takes time and practice. But that's why I'm here, to point you in the right direction and take time off your learning curve.

My rule of thumb?

Never hire the lowest bidder. In fact, more often than not, I go with the expert or organization that submits the highest bid.

Why?

Because they usually have the work record, experience, references, and samples to back them up.

Let someone else deal with the start-ups, the guys who don't have any experience. My time is too valuable to be wasted on outsourcers who might talk a solid game and then can't deliver the goods.

Now, let me be clear. We're talking right now about services and expertise, not products. So, for example, I'm all for bargain shopping on company vehicles, computer equipment, office supplies, and, heck, even hunting online promotional codes for discounts and free shipping. There's no shame in that game at all! If you can buy the same product at one store and pay less, obviously that's smart. In fact, let me give you three tools right this second that will help you do just that. When buying office supplies, computers, or any other business-related item, you'll definitely want to swing by price comparison websites like www.pricegrabber.com or www.mysimon.com. With a couple clicks of the mouse you will be able to quickly find the best price. Another cool place to check out is www.fatwallet. com. And, as an extra bonus, let me also suggest you click over to www.couponmom.com to bring down that grocery bill. See there, I told you I wasn't against pinching pennies where it makes sense to do so!

But what I don't like to see is when my students do what Dan Kennedy warns against, which is to miss opportunities because of price sensitive stupidity. As Dan likes to put it, "Don't step over dollars to pick up pennies." Dan's right. It's bad business and it always comes back to bite you in the butt.

> *I buy expensive suits. They just look cheap on me.* —Warren Buffett

When I was still a firefighter, everyone on my team recognized that we all had our strengths, from how we fought the fires to how we handled the pressures of the job and family to how we prepared while we were back at the station and what we did during the downtime.

One night, we were discussing this over dinner, and one of my fellow firefighters told us a funny story.

A friend of his who had recently finished a Ph.D. in Engineering Science at Penn State was driving home from a party when his car broke down at 3 a.m. If you've ever been there, you know that State College, Pennsylvania, is in the middle of nowhere, and he was on a back road 20 miles from the nearest small town. He didn't have AAA, so he called information and got the numbers of two drivers in the area.

The first told him he would be there in 30 minutes and it would cost him $200 to get to town. He would park the car in his own garage for the night and take it to the mechanic the next morning. When they got to town, he would be happy to drive the man home, which was 10 miles in the other direction.

The second driver told him he could be there in 15 minutes and it would cost him $100. No mention of where his car would be parked for the night or how he would get home. The friend told the second driver to come pick him up. After all, saving $100 can't be a bad thing, right?

Wrong!

The driver showed up two hours later. He was drunk. Despite refusing to ride with him or to have his car towed, the friend paid the man the agreed-upon hundred bucks just to get him to go away.

When he called the first driver after 6 a.m., the man laughed.

"You must have talked to Ike Colby after you talked to me, eh?" It wasn't the first time he'd gotten that second call to come and clean up after Ike Colby.

True to his word, the man showed up 30 minutes later—on the dot—and did exactly what he said he would do when he had been contacted three hours earlier.

All told, my colleague's friend spent $300 and didn't get home until 8 a.m., tired and a little bit smarter.

The irony wasn't wasted on him, of course. Ph.D. stud had gotten schooled. He laughed about it later, but he had learned a lesson.

What can you do to ensure that your outsourcing is productive and will save you time and money in the long run?

Do your due diligence and don't get ripped off. But realize that hiring experts is often the quickest way to spring ahead—and it's becoming part of the fabric of doing business every day.

STOP!

Put down this book and go to www.marchrisko.com. Just type your name and email address into the box on the left side of the page and I'll send you my new e-book, The 7 Fatal Mistakes Wannabe Millionaires Make ($47 value) ABSOLUTELY FREE!
Do it RIGHT NOW!

"Independent retailers who aren't charging customers for their expertise had better get started," says Mike McCurry, chairman of McCurry Associates. Twenty years ago, expertise was considered part of the purchase price. That is not the world we live in anymore. If you have a problem using Word or Excel or PowerPoint, you can't call Bill Gates and ask how to use it. The consumer is paying for expertise. They recognize the value of it."[22]

It took me a while to realize that small thinkers fear hefty price tags because they subconsciously don't think they'll ever be able to make enough money to pay them. That alone should prompt people to buy higher priced items to break down the mental barriers buried in their brains.

You can't be afraid to buy, or you will never be able to sell.

Let me say that again: *You can't be afraid to buy, or you will never be able to sell.*

The sooner you break down the mental barriers to high prices, the sooner you'll be able to justify raising your own.

I can relate, because I was one of the people who feared high-priced assistance. Learn a lesson from me and realize that what seems like a "high price" to you now is actually a steal in disguise.

TAKE ACTION NOW!

- Reject a low-dollar mindset on the services and strategic counsel that can rocket your business. Time is money. Be smart enough to shave years off your learning curve so you can get to your goals quicker.

- Seek the best. Use the best. Forget the rest.

- Trust yourself, trust your expert.

- *Become* the expert! Be willing to share your knowledge and skills to help others along. There's no limit on how many successful people can inhabit the planet. Do your part to increase the number. Make your knowledge and expertise available to others so that they might grow and experience the success you do.

Insiders Have Access to Bigger Players

You know the old saying: "I would never join any club that would have me."

Kind of funny. But the farthest thing from the truth.

You crave being on the inside, because that's where the action is, where the players hang out. And that's where every successful person wants—and needs—to be.

Why do successful people join country clubs? Sure, a lot of them like to play golf (you know, "Luxuriate Your Daily Lifestyle," Chapter 4). Or their families like the pool and the tennis courts. But even more important than taking advantage of the fun things clubs offer, players understand that *access is power*.

Why are some Hollywood producers more sought-after than others? Because they can deliver the actors, secure the funding, leverage their contacts in the industry so that the film gets green lighted.

Why do so many Major League free agents sign with the Yankees? Because they're making more money, sure. But they also know that when they go to New York, they're going to a team whose reputation for success and professionalism is second to none—and New York is a place where things get done.

Scott Boras is known as a Superagent to professional athletes. Why? Well, because for more than two decades, he's been doing the biggest deals in the sports world, and players know he'll go to bat for them, fighting tooth and nail for everything they deserve.

They also know that, with his unmatched connections in the advertising and A-list worlds, their name is going to be more prominent, endorsements more frequent, and celebrity greater with him than with any other agent.

Case in point: In 1985, Boras brokered a deal with the Toronto Blue Jays for a little-known 28-year-old relief pitcher named Bill Caudill. The former A's pitcher was hesitant to play in Canada, but Boras got him a deal worth about $8.7 million over five years—good money then, but lousy by today's standards (it takes Dodgers' outfielder Manny Ramirez and New York Yankees slugger Alex Rodriguez about 50 games to make what Caudill did in five years).

The important point, though, is Boras didn't quit there.

He had written into Caudill's contract that his player would be allowed to use his Blue Jays jersey for endorsement purposes. No other player on the team—and few in the league—had ever asked for such a clause.

Being on the inside has its advantages. Aligning yourself with people who know how to get things done is invaluable to your success.

Boras has done the same many times since for clients who are among the most popular and influential in sports and entertainment. He's brokered more than a dozen contracts of $60 million or more, and his office in Florida sounds more like a multi-media empire than the dream of a guy who traded in a minor-league baseball career to represent other players: 45 employees, a 23,000-square-foot office complex, 32 television receivers, 43 desks, and 70 flat-screen TVs, all so Boras can keep an eye on what's going on in the sports world and make the best decisions for his client.

All part of being on the inside.

Need further proof?

Boras was the one who negotiated Alex Rodriguez's 10-year $252 million contract with the Texas Rangers a few years back.[23]

But the example of Bill Caudill set a precedent for Boras's shrewd, hard-edged dealing.

Every client knows the true value of dealing with an insider. And every player who hires Scott Boras as their agent knows that, despite the fact that he's getting 15% or more of their income, he's worth every penny.

It's all about return on investment. Power breeds power.

You've heard the term rainmaker.

Rainmakers are the magnets, the people who just have a knack for attracting attention, big clients, money—POWER.

Author Russ Mountain lists some of the characteristics of the rainmakers you want to have on your team: "They have a historical successful track record that is easily verifiable and quantifiable. They know what they did and how. They can speak specifically to the impact and the results. Their background is filled with specific examples of multiple instances and situations where they reached specific high goals that they set, or accepted the responsibility for that required thoughtful planning, utilization of all available resources, massive effort, overcoming obstacles, rebounding from mistakes, and making few of them."

Sound like anyone you know? Sound like someone you'd like to *get* to know?

How important is it to align yourself with the best and the brightest?

Mountain tells a story about former General Electric CEO Jack Welch, who inherited the reins from his predecessor during a down market and turned GE into the global giant it is today.

The most important attributes for Welch when hiring his "rainmakers?" Authenticity, vision, resilience, and the ability to surround themselves with good people.[24]

The closer you are to power players the more likely you are to become one. Once you're in an Inner Circle of likeminded and ambitious, successful people, the truth is that one person doing you a personal favor or leveraging a personal contact of theirs will often pay for the entry fee into that particular group.

Like anything else in life, ambition goes a long way towards helping you to reach your goal.

Ask yourself these simple questions:

- What group do I want to join?

- What can I gain from belonging to that group?

- What can I offer in return?

- How can I best position myself to be invited?

- How can I make the most of my opportunity?

Keep your eyes on the prize, keep your ears open, and keep making contacts. Listen more than you speak. Take notes more than you lecture.

Choosing the company you keep will be one of the most important decisions you will ever make. Choose wisely.

Believe me, it's money well spent. Joint venture partners and affiliates take care of one another. By tapping into well-connected groups you are tapping into powerful reservoirs of connections and associations with other influential people.

TAKE ACTION NOW!

- You want to be on the inside. You *need* to be on the inside. That's where millionaire ideas and strategies reside. More importantly, that's where wealth-building relationships are forged.

- Find a star. Then become part of his constellation. Failure is certain for those without mentors.

- Don't be afraid to pay to play. The benefits will far outweigh the costs and zoom down the Kangaroo Millionaire path much, much quicker. Counterintuitive? Yes. True? You better believe it.

- Become a star!

Dribs and Drabs Drains Profits—Go Big

You know who annoys me most?

Those folks who sign up for all the free teleseminars, the free e-books, the free goodies, and then fail to take the next step and invest in themselves and their business but instead whine and complain when they fail to see a successful outcome.

Is it possible to inch along in dribs and drabs and eventually, years later, spring ahead in life and wealth? Sure, it's possible. But more likely than not, even if you're successful at keeping your head above water for a few years while chipping away at the available market, the longer you wait, the less your chance of going big.

Hey, there's nothing wrong with maintaining a mom-and-pop store for a few extra bucks. But if that's your intention, you're reading the wrong book.

If you want to grow by leaps and bounds you have to take massive action and never look back—kind of like the kangaroo.

According to the "Hot 100" league, which ranks entrepreneurial success, almost two-thirds of the fastest-growing companies were started by entrepreneurs who had taken out a second mortgage on their homes in order to finance their dreams. [25]

Little-known scientific fact: Kangaroos are incapable of moving backward.

Maybe that's why they go so fast when they're in drive!

But it's true. Kangaroos are physically incapable of hopping in reverse. They can only move in one direction and that's straight ahead. No matter their circumstances, kangaroos cannot move backwards.

When my Kangaroo spurred me to action, I never doubted that I would be successful. I moved ahead.

Find your Kangaroo—the person, knowledge, and systems that will produce millionaire income. And when you do, you have to go big or go home.

You have to leap and not look back. What lies ahead is far more amazing than anything that lies behind.

TAKE ACTION NOW!

• Get serious about your millionaire future. Commit to two to three years rigorously pursuing your millionaire destiny. Isn't it worth at least that much effort?

• Put your money where your dreams are. Invest in your education and the tools necessary to make your first million. The first mentor program I joined cost me over half of what I made a year as a firefighter, and within less than two years I was a millionaire. I'd say that's a pretty darn good ROI, wouldn't you?

• Going all in lets you hit the ground running. Go big or go home! The goal is to accelerate wealth, not piddle around. Kangaroo Millionaires bound toward their goal—and they don't dilly dally around. Get moving already! GO!

• Start each day with a commitment to springing forward with maximum velocity. Others will follow your lead. The best way you can help others is by showing them the folly in foot dragging. Spring hard and fast into the future and you'll show others the path to millionaire success and financial and personal freedom.

Like Attracts Like

The so-called "Law of Attraction" asserts that we become what we think about.

But if that were true, as Dan Kennedy says, all men would be women!

I, too, have some ethical problems with telling people that all outcomes are a function of their thoughts. Children with Leukemia, for example, obviously didn't *will* their cancer into being. I realize that's not what proponents of the Law of Attraction are really asserting, but that's my point: people can twist an idea until it loses all its meaning.

But one thing I think the Law of Attraction does a good job of doing is getting us to think about how what we surround ourselves with drives what we become.

Why do parents care so much about whom their kids hang around with? Because peer influences shape decision-making.

Take advertising, for example. Why would advertisers spend over $200 billion—with a B—dollars a year on advertising? They do it because they know that what we see and hear influences what we do.

As a popular story for advertisers goes, Philip K. Wrigley was on a flight to Chicago when the man next to him asked the chewing-gum magnate why he continued to advertise his product when it was the most popular in the world. Everyone knew the Wrigley brand.

"For the same reason that the pilot keeps this plane's engines running even though we're 30,000 feet in the air," Wrigley replied.

Surrounding yourself with like-minded people is a little like that jet. You don't really need the engines when you're sitting on the tarmac, but if you want to get anywhere fast, they had better be running smoothly.

Likewise, you need to begin enmeshing yourself in mastermind groups that contain a carefully selected mixture of successful people who think big. Actually, those two phrases describe the same thing: successful people think big, and big thinkers are successful people.

> *The essential element in personal magnetism is a consuming sincerity—an overwhelming faith in the importance of the work one has to do.* —Bruce Barton

Social networks, the free flow of ideas, and tips and shortcuts that save massive money and time are all benefits and outgrowths of joining a mastermind group. The concept of mastermind groups was developed by Napoleon Hill, researcher of the secrets to wealth acquisition and author of the classic in its field, *Think and Grow Rich*.

Nearly a century ago, Hill interviewed steel magnate Andrew Carnegie, then the richest man in the world, and came away with "a magic law of the human mind, a little known psychological principle" that would change the way that entrepreneurs would think about making money.[26]

Part of that success comes from the synergy—when the sum is greater than the parts—that occurs when groups of like-minded people get together for a common purpose. Hill defines the group as "the coordination of knowledge and effort of two or more people, who work toward a definite purpose, in the spirit of harmony...No two minds ever come together without creating a third, invisible intangible force, which may be likened to a third mind."

Sometimes, the most obvious example works the best. Bill Gates, the wealthiest person on the planet for more than a decade running, may have raised some eyebrows in his own family when he dropped out of Harvard in 1975. His parents thought he might be a lawyer, so they probably forgave him for choosing as he did.

But even as early as his prep days at Seattle's Lakeside School, Gates had decided to pursue a career in computers. He surrounded himself with others. Paul Allen and Ric Weiland — both of whom would become early employees of Microsoft and share in the company's remarkable success and wealth—were classmates of Gates. While at Harvard, he met Steve Ballmer, who would play a significant role in the company, as well as computer scientist Christos Papadimitriou.

They were all people who shared Gates's dream and who could appreciate his vision.

Who wouldn't give anything to have sat in on those early meetings? To see how the world's most successful business was built from the ground up? To observe how these like-minded visionaries met challenges and created systems that would be copied time and time again?

You can use the mastermind group (the term the legendary Napoleon Hill gave to gatherings of goal-oriented and influential people who conspire to help each other and themselves succeed) to your advantage even if you're not Bill Gates. In fact, today, you can get more information about such groups than ever before, because of ease of access (the Internet).

Listen, if you think the entry fee is steep, try the price tag of the learning curve. By taking the route I took, I cut years—not weeks, not months, but YEARS—off the typical learning curve for someone entering the real estate market.

So find your KANGAROO and bound into the future!

TAKE ACTION NOW!

- Set your sights on that which you wish to become.

- Paint a picture of the ideal you on your mental canvas. Your picture will become your reality, but only if you take action and heed the counsel of mentors who care about your success.

- Right now, write down the five "money magnets" that attract you. Commit to studying them and partnering with someone who can teach you the relative strengths and weaknesses of the various approaches to wealth creation.

- Become a magnet for others! What's the point of achieving success if you can't share it with others? Nothing is more enjoyable than shepherding another person to pursue and achieve their entrepreneur dreams. Nothing is more fulfilling than being someone else's Kangaroo.

Quality Reveals Itself

The operator of a small town hair salon was confident in the knowledge that his was the only salon in town. In fact, he was responsible for cutting and styling the hair of just about everyone in town. The money just rolled in.

Unfortunately, however, one day right across the street from his little hair salon sprang up one of those new full-service salon franchises. Its high-powered advertising campaign proclaimed, "EVERYTHING FOR $10! $10 haircuts, $10 perms, everything for $10."

Soon all his customers—even his neighbors—began patronizing the cut-rate salon across the street, and the man's once profitable business took a nosedive.

In desperation, he hired a big-city business consultant, saying to him, "I'm finished. How in the world am I going to compete with that big outfit with all that advertising and with those kind of prices?"

The consultant stood looking at the cut-rate salon across the street for several minutes, and watching the patrons pour in. Then, without saying anything to his desperate client, he picked up the phone and dialed the town's only billboard company.

"Yes," he said, "right on top of our building. In the biggest letters you can find, and do it right away.

"And make the message read: WE FIX $10 HAIRCUTS!"

It's a cute story with a serious point: Quality (or a lack thereof) always reveals itself. Invest in the best.

I'm fortunate enough to own a Rolex, a very nice watch that I bought as a reminder to myself what it took to get me to where I am today. I plan on having that watch for the rest of my life. Someday, my children will inherit it, and you can bet that they'll know the story behind it.

An associate of mine bought himself a Mont Blanc fountain pen on the day he sealed his first big deal. He'll have the reminder of that day for the rest of his life, every time he signs another contract or writes a letter to a loved one.

Another friend bought a flawless 1957 Chevy, a tribute to the year he was born, when he had made enough money to justify the purchase. It was significant that he didn't buy a brand-new Mercedes, for example, because new cars lose their value quickly. He has that classic Chevy 15 years later, and like the Rolex and the Mont Blanc, he'll pass that car down to his family when he's gone.

I've mentioned a number of things that have not only monetary value, but significance above and beyond cost. That's what *quality* is all about. Not just value, *significance*.

But these days, perception isn't always reality when it comes to high-end goods and services and how we think about them.

A buddy of mine told me a humorous but educational story about a Christmas gift his sister received as a gag gift one year. When she opened the box, she gasped with delight. It was a Rolex watch—the very thing that she had wanted from the time she was a little girl.

It looked like a Rolex, it ran like a Rolex—at least for a while—but the first time she tried to wind it, the stem broke off in her hand.

The joke was on her. What seemed to be her dream gift was, well, just the gag it was intended to be—a cheap knockoff sold for $20 on street corners.

More and more, you see the stories in the news, the fakes that turn up in all corners of the globe carrying names that you know—Gucci, Prada, Louis Vuitton, Fendi, Rolex. The list goes on.

In a 2007 story titled "Fakes—the new status symbols" in the *New Zealand Herald*, the extent of the problem becomes clear.

Altering one small aspect of the product is usually enough to keep intellectual property lawyers at bay, and the crime is often seen as victimless.

"Actress Renee Zellwegger has said that she bought a counterfeit bag in Hong Kong. She may not be the pinnacle of chic, but when multi-millionaire Britney Spears carries a pale-pink fake Chanel bag, tweens [between an adolescent and teenager] everywhere get the message that cheating the luxury good houses is cool."

The good news?

"Whether it's a knock-off handbag, a newsreader's youthful forehead or a trashy reality show, we've never been so accepting of fakes, and it's never been easier to falsify. But these days only the fool won't admit that they're faking it—because it has also never been easier to get caught."[27]

The sad fact is, not only do those products not have the same quality as the real thing, but they dilute the market, piggyback off of someone else's creativity, and take perceived value away from the real thing.

That's not only unfair in the marketplace, it's illegal.

Remember this: Quality will always reveal itself.

Maybe not immediately, but eventually.

This is especially true as it relates to education and specialized training. People who scrimp on their education often come to regret doing so, because the eventual costs will FAR outstrip the benefits.

What's wrong with going to college? Nothing. Nothing at all.

In many ways, colleges and universities are the backbone of our society: turning out educated people who will support the workforce for another generation and pass down important ideas to their children.

Most of my friends tried it—for at least a while—and many of them are doing well in their chosen professions. They're lawyers, doctors, contractors, businesspeople. But without wanting to sound boastful, I'm making more money in one year than they will make in ten.

If they're happy, I'm happy for them. I'm privileged to know some of the most intelligent and creative people any guy could ever know.

Maybe they fulfilled their parents' dream of seeing their son or daughter graduate from college and become "successful" and "respectful."

But in doing so, they paid several times more than I did for my training, and their return on investment is much lower (most of them are in their 30s and 40s and still chipping away at their student loans).

And that's my point: When it comes to making money, college isn't the way to go. As legendary media mogul Ted Turner once put it, "I didn't finish college because I couldn't afford to."[28]

We all make decisions about our lives generally and our finances specifically, and I'll choose financial security and peace of mind any day over a piece of paper to hang on the wall.

Why trust someone who doesn't know you well, know your goals and your strengths, with pointing you in the right direction?

Why assume that you'll make a good living by taking classes that have nothing to do with, well, making money?

Needless to say, my parents are as proud of me and my own family as they could be, and I know that, no matter what happens to me in the future, they'll be taken care of financially.

Why? Because I chose a path that combined quality of education with a ROI that can't be beat.

Knowing where to look is the first step.

Find your Kangaroo and leap.

TAKE ACTION NOW!

• Set high standards. Don't settle for anything less than the best.

• Buy an object of quality and keep it as a reminder of the commitment you've made to your future success.

• Put your business under the microscope and analyze its quality. Look for the weak links in your organization—and fix them!

• Hold your employees to the same standard of excellence that you hold yourself.

CHAPTER SIX

BE UNORIGINAL

New Is Seldom Better. Copy What Works

Ninety-nine percent of all surprises in business are negative. —Harold Geneen

What do you call something unoriginal? *Vanilla.*

You've heard that term referring to bland movies and television shows, lame football offenses, the everyday stuff that might strike you as, well, boring.

And I'll apply it to business, with one big difference: For me, vanilla isn't a four-letter word. I mean it as something tried-and-true, what-you-see-is-what-you-get, a flavor that goes with lots of other flavors.

Is vanilla boring? Maybe. Is it indispensable? You bet.

In fact, vanilla is the most popular ice cream flavor in the world.[29]

Despite what you've been told all your life, there's nothing wrong with being unoriginal. Boring and steady has made a whole lot more fortunes than "out there" and reckless.

Innovators imitate all the time. As the old saying goes, "Imitation is the sincerest form of flattery."

Richard Branson wasn't the first entrepreneur to start an airline, but his combination of marketing, convenience, and personality meant that the sky was the limit.

Ted Turner and Rupert Murdoch weren't the first media moguls to have grand visions for their empires, but they were innovators when it came to how people received their information. Now, it's hard to think about cable news and entertainment without CNN, TBS, and the FOX Network.

Donald Trump wasn't the first guy to think big when it came to real estate. But he was one of the first to make himself a business celebrity—and several billion dollars in the process.

Accumulating that kind of wealth isn't boring, it's just plain smart.

And that's the point: Unoriginal works.

Originality Is Overrated

Remember that annoying kid in school whose need for attention meant he just *had* to be different?

If everyone drank Coke, he drank Pepsi. If everyone looked up, he looked down. If the class fell silent, he shouted.

It wasn't genuine uniqueness, it was a gimmick. A silly ploy designed to try to stick out.

He dressed to stand out in a crowd, maybe wore orange Chuck Taylor high-tops to graduation and taped a sign to the top of his cap that said, "Will work for food."

He stuck out all right. Like a sore thumb!

I see too many wannabe entrepreneurs making the same mistake.

They think the only good ideas are those that no one has thought of before. Nothing could be further from the truth. In fact, there aren't that many original ideas out there, and most of them aren't that good!

Even Thomas Edison, probably the greatest inventor ever, failed more than 2,000 times before he had success with his most famous creation, the light bulb.

A lot of people have done innovative things with light bulbs since—fluorescent bulbs, headlamps in cars, energy-saving compact fluorescent bulbs, and a million others—and they didn't have to reinvent the wheel to make it happen. They reaped the substantial rewards of innovating rather than inventing.

Led Zeppelin, one of the most popular rock groups in history, owned the 1970s, selling out 80,000-seat venues, flying in their own jet, and influencing a generation of musicians.

Where did Robert Plant and Jimmy Page get their ideas?

From the rock-and-roll of their youth and the old blues masters, musicians like Robert Johnson, Muddy Waters, and others.

"It was the obvious influences at the beginning, Scotty Moore, James Burton, Cliff Gallup—he was Gene Vincent's guitarist—Johnny Weeks," guitarist Jimmy Page said in an interview.

"Those seemed to be the most sustaining influences until I began to hear blues guitarists Elmore James, B. B. King, and people like that. Basically, that was the start—a mixture between rock and blues."[30]

Led Zeppelin's music wasn't original, but it was innovative. And boy, did those guys turn out great music. Every one of their albums is still a classic.

> Some of the big boys always have funds that perform well year in, year out. They are not sexy, not like those funds that just do well for two or three years and then drop off. They are generally fairly boring companies, but they are far more likely to do well in the longer term. —Mark Dampier, head of research for Hargreaves Lansdown

Google wasn't the first Internet search engine—AltaVista and Yahoo both predate the world's most popular site by three years—but it's certainly the best-known. In 2006, after doubling the company's workforce in a single year, founders Larry Page and Sergey Brin were listed as two of the wealthiest people in the world, billionaires while still in their 20s.

Even they would admit that they didn't invent the mouse trap (or, in this case, the information trap), they just perfected it. And added a whole line of high-profile systems that keep users coming back.

In other words, they took a pre-existing product and used it to fulfill their vision, not the other way around.

History tells us that there will always be another Google, another Virgin, another FOX.

Look, the goal is to make buckets of money, not win a blue ribbon for originality. The simple fact is this: Business models and concepts that are completely new have no track record, no precedents, no entrepreneurial "blueprints" to follow.

That means if you're set on implementing a totally original idea, you're going to be flying solo. And that means you run a higher risk of wasting money trying to reinvent the wheel. Conversely, going with a proven winning wealth strategy is smart because success leaves traces. Success leaves hints and clues that can be replicated.

If you can deliver the goods, people don't care if you're breaking new ground or not. In fact, they'd probably rather that you didn't do it on their time—and at their expense—if one of your "original" ideas didn't pan out.

Just look at how many billionaires are in boring, old industries that made a lot of people a bunch of money.

Remember, there are no original ideas, only variations on the ones already out there. Sometimes we strain so hard to find what is already right in front of us staring us in the face.

A great example of that involves the master escape artist and magician Houdini. Houdini always proudly proclaimed that he could escape from anything.

During a tour of Scotland, Houdini agreed to be locked up in the strongest jail cell available, boasting that he would escape from it.

The magician was searched, his hands placed in steel handcuffs, and he was chained to a bench in the jail cell. The jailer shut the cell door and walked away, confident that Houdini would never escape.

Left alone, Houdini quickly shed himself of the handcuffs and the chain binding him to the bench. Then he went to work on the cell door.

He tried every trick in the book to pick the lock on the jail house door. After an hour he was dripping with sweat, apparently defeated. Totally discouraged, and near exhaustion, Houdini accidentally leaned against the door and it swung open easily, sending him tumbling into the corridor. The jailer had forgotten to lock the door.

The moral is that you can waste a lot of time and energy trying to open an unlocked door or solve a problem that somebody else has already solved.

So stop wasting time trying to come up with some Houdini-like original idea on how to escape from your financial handcuffs. Find a proven money-making system and get to work NOW!

Bottom line: *originality is overrated.*

TAKE ACTION NOW!

- Unoriginal isn't bad. Often, it's smart. Identify consistent profit-centers with established track records.

- Identify three proven wealth builders with long-standing track records. Right now, list the advantages and disadvantages of each. Also, consider how long it will take to get educated on that business sector and how long it would take to raise the capital necessary to get up and running.

- Join a mastermind group in your area of interest. Surround yourself with proven winners in your area of wealth creation.

- Create similar mastermind opportunities for others. Become a mentor. Visit the Napoleon Hill Foundation's website for information on how to begin a mastermind group (www.naphill.org).

Take the Proven Paths

Here's the thing: You have to find the sectors that succeed time and time again. For me, that meant seizing opportunity in the most proven business of all: real estate. As long as people need homes, and businesses need land, real estate will continue to be white hot. This is ESPECIALLY true in the wake of the financial crisis and fallout from the subprime mortgage mess.

No matter where I go these days, I'm reminded of the downturn that has led to so many properties being on the market, many of them for well below their appraised value. It seems as though every other house in some neighborhoods has a FOR SALE sign in front of it. The classified ads in every city I visit on my many speaking engagements are filled with ads soliciting buyers for businesses that were booming just a year ago.

And do you know what that means for real estate investors like me?

It means we're in one of the best real estate cycles an entrepreneur could ever hope for. That's counterintuitive, which is part of the reason that you'll be so successful when you take advantage of the killer opportunities out there right now.

The deals are *everywhere*!

By October 2008, as the stock market continued to plummet, real estate sales were on the rise in the West, up 7% from July to August and surging. California, Nevada, and Arizona were all up more than 20%. Idaho was up a whopping 51% from the previous quarter![31]

What does this all mean?

Somebody will benefit from the current situation, and it may as well be YOU. As the old saying goes, "Buy when there's blood in the streets."

---

*We are what we repeatedly do. Excellence, then,
is not an act, but a habit.* —Aristotle

Why real estate and not, say, a popular food franchise?

Well, when my Kangaroo inspired me to pursue my kangaroo quest, I thought the same thing. I thought owning a franchise might be a proven winner. But the more research I conducted, the more amazed I became. It turns out that franchises don't come cheap, and the overhead can be a killer. Most franchises require an initial investment of six-figures or more, and you're probably going to end up paying royalties to the franchiser whether you're turning a profit or not. In today's economy, things could get ugly in a hurry for you if you're locked into a franchise deal in a market that's not doing well. And when you're selling a $1 hamburger, making a huge profit is, by definition, impossible.

Another thing that surprises most people to learn is that franchisers control you and your business from the sidelines. Even though you're the one putting in all the work—there's no being lazy when you operate a franchise—franchisers can make things difficult for you if you don't operate your business the way they want you to. This can include forcing you to buy products and services whether you need them or not.

And the most shocking dirty little secret of all is this: the average franchise contract locks you in for nearly 11 years! That's right, 11 years—one year less than it took you to get a high school diploma! Who has that long to wait to live the good life?! Not me! And all of this, despite a study showing that franchises are twice as likely to go out of business than existing independent small businesses.[32]

There's a reason Donald Trump, B. Francis Saul II, Richard LeFrak, and my inspiration and the creator of the Rich Dad brand of education, Robert Kiyosaki, chose to build their empires in real estate. Despite what the markets do, real estate is always a solid investment. (Even after 40 years in the business, Donald Trump, when asked what profession he would go into today, replied, "Real estate. I love it, and it still exists as a career and a viable passion."[33])

As a kid, I would go for weekend rides with my father. Any time we passed a plot of land or a house for sale, he would say, "Can't go wrong there. They don't make more land, you know."

His words stuck with me. And they've never been truer than they are today.

Now is the time for you to make your move.

Real estate appreciates faster than most stocks in the short term and is a more stable investment in the long term. Even in economic downturns, real estate is "stickier." That is, it depreciates at a slower rate than stocks and other investments.

For the five-year period beginning in 1999, real estate prices rose 56%, while the S & P 500 dropped nearly 6%.[34]

Between 2001 and 2006, stock prices rose on average 4.3% annually. Real estate came in at 12.4%.[35]

You do the math.

TAKE ACTION NOW!

- Don't pick what's sexy, pick what's proven to build profits.

- Determine your best investment opportunities by focusing on short-term returns and long-term stability.

- Do your research. What are the hot markets now, and what will they be in the near future? Go check out YouNoodle's networking for startups and valuation with Startup Predictor (www.younoodle.com).

- Own your investment. Don't let it own you.

Systems! Systems! Systems!

Michael Gerber's mega-bestselling book, *The E-Myth: Revisited*, drives home one central point: Entrepreneurial success depends upon your ability to implement and perfect SYSTEMS.

"Picture the typical entrepreneur and Herculean pictures come to mind: a man or woman standing alone, wind-blown against the elements, bravely defying insurmountable odds," Gerber writes, playing on our sense of the lone genius fighting to gain the recognition that he knows he must deserve for his brilliant idea. He continues, "Climbing sheer faces of treacherous rock—all to realize the dream of creating a business of one's own."[36]

The reality is something much less heroic.

As Gerber wisely points out, you need to keep in mind one very important thing, and everything else will fall into place: *Everything is a system*. "The universe, the world, San Francisco Bay, the office I'm sitting in, the word processor I'm using, the cup of coffee I'm drinking, the relationship you and I are having—they're all systems."[37]

Anything you do more than three times should be systematized, says productivity and time-management guru Laura Stack. And in her book, *The Exhaustion Cure*, she breaks down every aspect of daily life into a system. Things like sleep, diet, nutrition, exercise, relaxation, attitude, responsibilities, relationships—all the daily activities that make us who we are.

Systematizing your life sure makes things easier. If you commit yourself to putting efficient systems into place in your business, you can maintain your business with little effort and ensure that you continue to realize a return on your investment.

Time and money. The best of both worlds!

How many times have you solved a problem in a new way, just to find that, once you try to go back and do it again, you have no idea how you did it successfully the first time?

The classic example of an entrepreneur who understood the value of systems is Henry Ford. He figured out the basics of his assembly line, which began as a simple idea, as a young man.

After leaving home, the young tycoon-to-be worked in a machine shop, saving enough money to buy a three-dollar watch. Being the curious type, he took it apart as soon as he got home.

Pricing each part, Ford realized that if thousands of watches could be made in exactly the same way, the unit cost of the entire watch would be about 37 cents. Even when he added marketing expenses and his own profit, the final price would still be low enough for the watch to be affordable to everyone.

In other words, increasing his efficiency also greatly increased the potential market for his product.

Now that's genius!

When Ford got interested in automobiles, he remembered his early experience with the watch. By turning to mass production, he could push down his costs and earn small profits on each car sold at a price that would fit the budgets of most families.

By 1908, his Model T car carried a price tag of $840, while a car with every part hand-designed cost more than $9,000.

By 1926, the price of Ford's car dropped to $248. By that time, nearly 15 million Model T's had been sold, and the automobile had been converted from a luxury item for the rich to a replacement for the horse.

Ford's focus on systems can't be overrated. It revolutionized the way we think about business.

In fact, when you look today at the failures of so many businesses, both large and small, you can often point to the breakdown of systems as the main cause for that failure.

So here's what you need to do: Create a streamlined formulaic process that produces consistent and predictable results and ROI (in fact, everything you do should be focused on return on investment).

Whether you're talking about a pizza parlor or a portfolio manager, you need to have a system in place that dictates, step-by-step, how each stage of your work is to unfold.

Only then can you create passive streams of income as well as proven results that minimize risk.

Only then can you reach your potential as the most efficient and effective worker that you can be.

TAKE ACTION NOW!

- Stop thinking about your business as a collection of random details. You must make it a *system*. Coordinate your teammates and partners using the FREE collaborative project management tools over at Project2Manage (www. project2manage.com)or Zoho (www.zoho.com).

- Anything you do more than three times needs to be streamlined. Analyze your daily business activities and identify areas that can be systematized.

- Increase your efficiency by automating communication. Forms are your friend. Create templates and use them. Pop over to SurveyMonkey (www.surveymonkey.com) where you can create and publish custom online surveys and forms for FREE!

- Keep those to-do lists organized and automated. Go check out the cool tool with the funky title: Remember the Milk (www.reememberthemilk.com) for help with task management solutions and to-do lists.

Be a Winner by "Drafting" the Lead Cars

The idea of drafting in NASCAR was first introduced in 1960 by Junior Johnson, one of the sport's great characters and a former moonshiner who honed his driving skills while evading capture by the feds. At the Daytona 500 that year, Junior discovered that the only way his slower Chevrolet could keep up with the Pontiacs was if he rode close to the rear bumper of the car in front of him.

Toward the end of that race, the draft produced by Junior's car was so strong that it sucked the window out of the car ahead of him, allowing him to win.[38]

These days, the physics of drafting are much better understood, but the principle remains the same as it was 50 years ago: Getting in the "draft" of a successful person is the best way of getting into the game. It's also the one that uses the least energy and gives you an advantage over the competition.

Remember, you're trying to be lazy! Don't work any harder than you have to! The secret to drafting is finding a mentor— your KANGAROO—who has been down the road and knows all the entrepreneurial landscape in your area of business.

If you wish to know the road ahead, inquire of those who have traveled it. —Chinese proverb

---

"From the university of life to the ranks of the super-rich," an article published in the *Daily Mail* (London), details the remarkable record of Scots who either served time as apprentices or did vocational training. Twenty-one of the 100 richest people in Britain are in that group, including Sir Alex Ferguson, Billy Connolly, Jim McColl, William Haughey, and celebrity chef Gordon Ramsay (also the youngest, in his early 40s).

"On the UK list, the vast majority of entries are self-made, with only four out of 100 inheriting their wealth," Steven Henry writes, "and even these turned their family business into much larger enterprises. And their 'hands-on' approach to business is helping them hold off the financial squeeze."[39]

Ramsay is an interesting and informative case study. He's the popular and profane chef on top-rated cooking shows in the United States and Great Britain, including *Hell's Kitchen* and *Gordon Ramsay's Kitchen Nightmares*.

Ramsay can be such an abrasive character, at least in front of the camera, that it sounds odd to hear him admit that he has relied on someone else to keep him moving toward his goal. In Ramsay's case, that would be total domination of the world's high-dollar restaurant market. He already operates 18 world-class restaurants from New York to Tokyo to London to Los Angeles to Dubai and is recognized as one of the few celebrity chefs who earned his way to the top with hard, smart work and innovation.

Ramsay's mentor is his father-in-law, Chris Hutcheson. "He is an amazing figurehead," Ramsay says. "The guy grew up with no father. I had no father, but in the second stage of my life, he's been everything. Chris is incredibly focused; he has an amazing vision in business. As the secret ingredient he's a chef's dream because chefs make the world's worst businessmen."[40]

Let me tell you, I know the value of working with gurus firsthand. I didn't plunk down $80,000 on a college education, but I did pay over $35,000 to be mentored and coached by gurus who knew what they were talking about and how to slingshot me across the finish line in first place.

It was the best investment I ever made.

In fact, sometimes I feel guilty that I only paid $35,000 for information that has made me over 90 times as much in a single year. I shaved so many years off my learning curve simply by drafting off of cars who'd run the track millions of times and who knew all the best strategies and tactics.

You need to do the same.

But the way I repay and honor the gift my mentors and coaches gave me is to teach and share these principles with my students. Nothing provides me with greater satisfaction than to see them make more money in their first deal than they would make in a year. Being a Kangaroo to others and helping them find the financial freedom to spend time with their families and to cast away financial fear is a gift unlike any other. I hope it's something you experience one day as well.

TAKE ACTION NOW!

- Don't be afraid to be in the number two position. Drafting will slingshot you into the lead.

- Find your lead car (KANGAROO). Slingshot yourself to victory.

- Investment leads to success. Get in the race!

- Encourage others to draft off you. Create a legacy of leadership.

History Is the Greatest Teacher

In 2002, not long after the dot.com bubble burst, *Wired* magazine published an entire issue devoted to history. The subtitle of a feature piece called "Past Is Prologue" says it all: "The future is history. Rewind."

About the historic failure of the tech boom, the magazine took a wait-and-see approach. Someone had done their homework. There were no panicked calls for changing the way people invested or developed new products and services. Just a recognition that markets rise and fall, and that we needed to ride out that cycle.

"The truth is that our history is filled with bursts and busts. Freneticism and disappointment, excitement and fear: The cycles are familiar. History is bunk—right up until it repeats itself," the article proclaimed. "The Internet is just part of a stream of economic, cultural, and industrial revolutions that date back centuries. Each was amazing. Each was disruptive. All left both glory and chaos in their wake."[41]

In other words, appreciate the fact that you live when you do, but don't ever think that you're somehow free from the pull of history.

Sometimes, though, it's easy to get too locked into history. When that happens, unwillingness to change can be your worst enemy.

David K. Scott tells a story about Galileo's famous experiment and what it tells us about our relationship with history. In 1589, Galileo called the world's most learned men to the Leaning Tower of Pisa for a demonstration that would disprove a 2,000-year-old principle of physics. It was Aristotle who first claimed that the heavier an object, the faster it would fall to earth.

From the top of the tower, Galileo dropped a ten-pound and a one-pound weight. They landed at the same time.

The result?

Conventional wisdom was so powerful and change so threatening that the professors Galileo brought to the tower all denied what they had seen.

That experiment, done more than 400 years ago, still has practical applications today, Scott says.

You have to preach the truth to people who refuse to believe it, even after seeing it with their own eyes.

You need to understand the past in order to be able to make informed decisions about the future—and to trust those decisions.

Business is the same way.

Warren Buffett, the world's richest man, has a simple method for knowing where to invest his money. He reads the companies' own data to see how they've performed in the past and how they are projected to perform in the future.

> *I have but one lamp by which my feet are guided, and that is the lamp of experience. I know no way of judging the future but by the past. —Edward Gibbon*

Past performance doesn't always dictate what a company will do in the future, of course. But when you've seen as many stock reports as Warren Buffett has, you begin to see patterns where others don't. You start to trust your gut. Decision-making becomes second nature.

Profits soar, even in down markets.

Obviously Buffett has a trained eye—and brain—that can see what others can't. But that's the point. He studies in ways most people don't.

In an August 2008 interview with CNBC's *Squawk Box*, Buffett responded to the economic downturn with optimism for the future and the resolve of someone who has seen it all in more than 60 years of investing.

"You only find out who's been swimming naked when the tide goes out," Buffett remarked. "Well, we found out that Wall Street has been kind of a nudist beach."

When the "Oracle of Omaha," Warren Buffett, was asked how long the crisis might last, his response was both realistic and forward-looking. But it was also based on his vast and shrewd knowledge of what had come before.

"I've said in the past [the downturn] ought to be longer and deeper, and I think it is going to be longer and deeper, but no one knows when—what you do know is that it will turn around. I mean, the country will be doing far better five years from now than it is now, but it won't be, in my judgment, it won't be doing better five months from now."[42]

In other words, cooler heads will prevail, and if you think that's there no way to succeed in a down market, you're wrong.

Your pessimism will cost you dearly.

The only way you can lose by investing in America, Buffett says, is by trying to outsmart the market. That historical long-term view is what has kept him at the top of the game.

If you don't know what's worked in the past, how can you predict what will work in the future?

When writing about his experiences with the tribes of Alaska, anthropologist Marvin Harris uses knowledge of the past as an illustration of how goods and services can benefit from what has come before.

"What is the source of quality that one finds, let us say, in a Pomo Indian basket so tightly woven that it was used to hold boiling water and never leaked a drop. Or in an Eskimo skin boat with its matchless combination of lightness, strength and seaworthiness.

"Throughout history it was the fact that producers and consumers were either one and the same individuals or close kin, guaranteeing the highest degree of reliability and durability in manufactured items."

It wouldn't do, Harris writes, for a spearhead to fall off mid-flight, or a cold-weather parka to fail at -60 degrees.

As far as I'm concerned—and I'm speaking from my own experience here—the process of educating yourself is much the same.

You start with knowledge of the past and work your way up from there. And with the help of your KANGAROO, you'll get where you're going.

TAKE ACTION NOW!

- Study the past. It will determine your future.

- Study the ROI trajectories of your three potential investment markets.

- Invest in education specific to your chosen market. What you know determines how far you go.

- History is an indicator, not a predictor. Lead by example.

Clone Yourself

Being a KANGAROO MILLIONAIRE means taking quantum leaps toward the dream lifestyle.

What you need to realize, however, is that millionaire success can be a blessing or a curse. If you set up your systems in ways that demand your endless time and attention, then you will be shackled to your office and beholden to more people than you can possibly please.

If, however, you build and implement systems that yield consistent results and returns, you will be freed up to enjoy passive streams of income that run virtually on autopilot.

Which one would you rather have? Kind of a no-brainer.

So that means maximizing the advantages technology offers. For example, you might create a Camtasia video (Screen Flow if you are a Mac user like me) of your training session so that you don't have to waste time saying the same things over and over and over again when training a new recruit.

Another thing you can do right this second is to set up a Jott account (www.jott.com) so you can blast out a message via your cell phone to the inboxes of several members of your team, all with one simple phone call that transcribes your voice message into text.

Finally, why not buy a digital recorder so you can shoot messages to your colleagues via an emailed iTunes-style recording? Personally, I like the Olympus WS-300M. You hit "Record," talk into it, plug it into your computer, and presto! It creates an MP3 audio file that you can email as an attachment. Super easy to use and costs $99. It's hard to beat. Best of all, you will save yourself the one thing you can't create more of—time—when you learn the entrepreneurial art of cloning yourself.

So hurry up and get hopping!

TAKE ACTION NOW!

• Motion needs to be controlled. Being busy doesn't necessarily mean being productive.

• Create an information product that allows you to be in more than one place at a time. For example, you can host a FREE conference call or teleseminar by using services like Free Conference (www.freeconference.com) or others. For a small fee they will even record your call so you can turn it into an audio CD or other digital product.

• Use technology to broaden the reach of your message and get your team on the same page. Utilize project management tools such as Basecamp (www.basecamphq. com) which allows you to organize projects so that your team can work remotely and efficiently.

• Don't muddle your message. Simplify. Clear and crisp— that's how you want your communications.

CHAPTER SEVEN

GIVE STUFF AWAY

Generosity is a Boomerang

*We make a living by what we get. We make a life
by what we give.* —Winston Churchill

When the richest man on planet earth dies, 85% of his massive $63 billion dollar empire will be going straight to charity.

So much for the stereotype of the old, rich, greedy miser!

In 2007, Warren Buffett shocked the world when he announced that he would be giving away his gigantic piggy bank to the Bill and Melinda Gates Foundation.

Indeed, when you start looking closely at the lives of the affluent, you begin to notice a startling trend: most are extremely generous.

Now, sure, there may be critics out there who quip, "Well, sure they're generous. They want a fat tax right off! And besides, they've got tons of dough to blow, so what do they care anyhow?"

That kind of jealous thinking exists, and it's unfortunate. It also happens to be absolutely wrongheaded.

Here's a provocative hypothesis: Maybe—just maybe—one of the secrets of the mega-wealthy is that they realize that generosity is a boomerang.

It's true. What we give we get.

Now, that's not the motivation for giving. Nor should it ever be.

But I will tell you this much, every time I give generously I get paid back in spades—spiritually, emotionally, and, yes, often financially.

Why? Well, it's because giving to others teaches you to let go of wealth and builds the confidence that you will always build more. It also helps you to understand and absorb the principle of serving others. And what is a business if not an organization that is dedicated to serving other people called "customers" and meeting and exceeding their needs?

Really go back and think about that last sentence. It will unlock new vistas of leadership within you.

Now, I realize that there are some money "gurus" who will tell you to grip every last penny like it's your last. They will say that what I've just told you is silly and overly spiritual. They will tell you to wrench every last dime you can out of a customer and to never budge when brokering a deal. I know that that thinking exists. It's unfortunate that it does. But the reason I vehemently disagree with that outlook on life and wealth has nothing to do with morals or ethics (although I find it incredibly disturbing on both of those levels). No, the reason I take strong objection to that mentality is because…well, it's just plain bad business.

Stingy is Stupid

The minute you suspect someone is selfish and self-centered, what do you do? You throw up a wall. You watch your back. You keep your hand gripped tightly around your wallet. Why? Because stingy people are looking to squeeze every last penny out of others and business deals. You have to be willing to leave something on the table; always strive to create win-win scenarios. If you don't give you will never get. Generosity gains far more than it loses. Stingy is stupid.

As the old saying goes, "Pigs get fed, hogs get slaughtered." Kangaroo Millionaires understand this because they reject a scarcity mindset. Look, it's not like there is a limited number of people who are permitted to become 7-figure earners in the world. There's plenty of room for everyone to flourish. So why be guarded and stingy about your resources and knowledge? I never understood that about some would-be entrepreneurs. They act as though there are a limited number of people who can become successful and they are gripping their ticket with every muscle in their bodies.

> *No one has ever become poor by giving. —Anne Frank*

Now, again, I realize that there are a lot of people—even some in my industry—who criticize me for giving away too much information in my books and seminars. "Knock it off, Hrisko!" they grouse. "You're giving away the farm for free! You're making us all look bad. Stop it!" Look, I've heard it all before. I hear this stuff frequently.

But you know what I say to that? Let them complain. I had nothing when I started. I remember what it was like to be clueless and unsure of whom I could trust. I was a firefighter with a high school diploma and big dreams and empty pockets. I resolved long ago that when I made my first million—not "if" but "when"—I would do all I could to lift others up, not tear them down. Sure, success is ultimately an individual endeavor, but it takes finding your Kangaroo—the education, mentors, and systems that create and sustain wealth—to spring a person forward toward millionaire status. And that's what I decided I wanted to be: Other people's "Kangaroo," just as my wife had been to me.

Do I give away more "content" and "strategies" than probably makes financial sense to do so? Yes. Do I give a rip what others think about that? No, I don't. The reality is that you are more likely to trust me as your millionaire coach if you know that I rain down massive quantities of valuable, actionable, real content and strategies on my students.

Think about it. When, for example, I give away $47 reports or e-books for FREE, or when I give away my $97 audio course for nothing more than the cost of shipping, you see that and think to yourself, "Well geez…if his FREE content is this good, I can't IMAGINE how amazing his paid materials and coaching must be! MAN, I want to buy everything this guy has to sell. Give me everything you have to sell!"

Do you see my point? Giving others massive value isn't stupid, it's the smartest thing one can do. Not just because it makes me feel good or reflects a generous spirit (although it does both), but because it makes good business sense, too.

Let's face it. The world is small and getting smaller. People talk. Treat a client poorly and the Internet is humming with chatter about it. Act shady in a business deal and you'll find it plastered across newspaper headlines or multiplying at Mach speed on blog postings. The point is that being miserly and piggish is hardly a path to millionaire wealth. It's hard to root for people whose values others abhor.

TAKE ACTION NOW!

- Reject a scarcity mindset. There's plenty of prosperity for everyone to pursue. Get out of the small mindset that thinks that there is only one golden ring and that you have to muscle others out of the way to grab it. That's counterproductive and small. Worse, it doesn't build within you the mind of a millionaire.

- Volunteer your time to a cause that moves you. There's no better way to sharpen your entrepreneurial instincts than to keep yourself acutely aware of meeting the needs of others. That's what business owners do. So click over to www.volunteermatch.com and find the cause that speaks to your soul and get off your butt and get involved.

• Get in the habit of giving away massive quantities of value to prospects and clients. Don't fall prey to the belief that you should "hold back the good stuff." That's ridiculous. If people implement what you tell them and find success, where do you think they will turn to continue their growth and development? Duh! To you!

People Root for Benevolence

When you give, you show others that you can be trusted to do business with. They see that you have the values and priorities that make them trust you and feel good about giving you their trust and business. And nothing is more important to building your brand and what it stands for.

The Kangaroo Millionaire mentality understands that your company and your brand translate into an emotional meaning in the hearts and minds of your clients or customers. When you see a brand logo, for example, whether you realize it or not, you have an emotional reaction inside yourself. Sometimes the reaction is based on an experience you had with the product. Other times it has to do with the way you were treated in their stores. And still other times it's about the way their advertising makes you feel. But the point is this: Brands mean something. Human beings interact with brands the way they do with people—emotionally.

> *Think of giving not as a duty but as a privilege.* —John D. Rockefeller, Jr.

Now ask yourself: What kind of emotion do I want surging through my customers' and clients' hearts and minds when they see my brand or hear my company's name?

If you think about it, whatever answer you gave, showcasing your generosity would only stand to *improve* and *amplify* that image, not reduce it. And perhaps that's the easiest way for you to think of it: There is zero downside to generosity, there are plenty of pitfalls that can come with being tightfisted.

Winning fans means laying it all on the line and demonstrating your passion and heart in the way you conduct and run your business and personal life. So be wise and be generous. They're one in the same.

The goal is to make giving a "movement." Create business launches and promotional efforts that center around philanthropy. It's easy and fun and will build your brand in ways you can't possibly imagine. You will find that when you begin a movement people—regular folks, powerful folks, even famous folks—all start to come out of the woodwork. It's really something to behold. But people from all backgrounds and walks of life will begin to converge and assimilate around you and your cause. Some will pitch in because they like you and your business. Others will join the cause through word of mouth. And still others will have had some personal experience or challenge that drives them to want to lend a helping hand. But the point is that giving will become a movement that sparks a wildfire of potential and opportunity, and all while doing real work that can transform real lives.

So host a charity golf tournament. Create a "work FREE for a day" campaign by partnering with other businesses. Make a competition out of it. Have fun!

TAKE ACTION NOW!

• Donate $50 right this second. Hop online and donate money to a charity that you're passionate about. Learn to let the generosity boomerang fly. The sooner you do, the sooner it will come back around.

• When a brother firefighter of mine told me about his grandson's battle with autism, it sparked a passion in me to help support autism research and support for families of autistic children. Find a person you care about with an existing challenge or need and get involved. This gives a "face" to the cause and will motivate you to work that much harder and give that much more generously, both in your time and finances.

• Start a movement. Align it with your business or niche. For example, if you are in sporting goods, host a golf tournament. If you are in the restaurant business, why not cater lunch to a battered and abused women's shelter? Find a need and meet it. Get creative. Be spontaneous.

Reciprocity is Real

Look on the cover of this book.

Do you see that red sunburst sticker on the cover? What's it say?

That's right, it says you're getting $297 worth of materials for FREE.

Why would I give things away that are worth over 10 times the price of the book? It's because I know it's all coming back to me. You're going to be far more likely to want me to mentor and coach you if I prove that I always over-deliver and provide you with ten times the content and value than you pay for.

Better still, it tells you that I'm a sincerely and genuinely generous person who would rather see you succeed than to trick you into buying crap.

That's called the Law of Reciprocity.

Think about it.

When you get a gift from someone, what's the first thing you do? That's right, you give them something in return. Perhaps out of a sense of obligation, perhaps to be polite, or perhaps because you genuinely wish to show your gratitude.

But the point is you give something back when you get something.

Now, how much more so when you receive something of genuine and significant worth from someone who expects little if nothing in return?

Do you see how that works? The more value you give others, the more they will want to return the favor.

> Real generosity toward the future lies in giving
> all to the present. —Albert Camus

Now, let me be clear. Kangaroo Millionaires NEVER give solely to get. That's insincere and phony, and people will sense it. Plus, that's operating from a scarcity mindset, and that's a no-no.

But if you want to explode your entrepreneurial endeavors you will master and practice the Law of Reciprocity in all you do.

When you have a phone session with a prospect or client, make sure to come armed with an informational goodie, a nugget that will make the other person money.

When you send a client or prospect an email, add in a P.S. at the bottom and send them a link to a new FREE widget or online tool that you think will help them achieve their goals and increase their productivity. Again, the value of saving other people the time to find and collect these kinds of pieces of information gold is invaluable. That's why you may have noticed that I've peppered this entire book with website addresses to AMAZING free tools that will jumpstart your Kangaroo Millionaire journey. The point is that by giving to others you are building a reputation as a genuine and generous individual who cares more about others and *their* success than in what you can weasel out of people.

TAKE ACTION NOW!

- Learn more about the Law of Reciprocity by reading the classic book *Influence* by Robert Chaldini.

- Go grab a file folder right now and write "AMAZING FREE GOODIES" on the tab. Then, any time you find an amazing online resource or tool, print out a copy of the homepage and drop it in your file. Get in the habit of adding one of these goodies into the postscript (P.S.) of your emails to new and existing clients and friends.

- Always read newspaper and magazine articles with an eye toward stories that might be useful to your clients and prospects. There's nothing cooler than getting a letter in the mail with a newspaper or magazine clipping with a handwritten note attached that says, "I read this article and it struck me as powerful information that you could use. Happy reading!"

Find the 'Roo' In YOU!

I began this book with a confession, so I think it's only appropriate that I end with one as well.

I wrote this book with a massive ulterior motive in mind, and here it is: I want you to discover the 'Roo' in YOU!

I want you to discover that you can become a Kangaroo for others—a mentor who teaches others the knowledge, strategies, and systems every entrepreneur must master on their path toward millionaire success.

My wife was and is my Kangaroo. She jolted me into action and helped me find the resources I needed to pursue and achieve a seven-figure lifestyle. But here's the thing: Very few people ever find their Kangaroo.

It's sad but true.

There's no greater reward than helping ignite the spark in others that sets them springing ahead in life and wealth. Our lives are about what we give to others. It's about serving people and helping them meet and exceed their dreams.

As a firefighter, I was blessed to help protect others in times of danger and tragedy. Today, I am blessed to help people grow their businesses and achieve the financial freedom they desire and deserve.

I want you to know and feel the joy I experience on a daily basis. I want you to become a Kangaroo to others, especially those whom you love. There is no greater feeling than to know that you have shared knowledge that will transform the lives of others. I want you to find the 'Roo' in YOU!

TAKE ACTION NOW!

- Once you're done with this book, share it with your friends and family members. Doing so may be just the nudge they need to get hopping down the Kangaroo Millionaire trail.

- Develop and refine your leadership and teaching skills by joining a mentorship group. My Kangaroo Millionaire Tribe is an elite group of go-getters who are ready to take massive action and commit to a rigorous hands-on experience to add rocket fuel to their millionaire journey. The Kangaroo Millionaire Tribe is NOT right for everyone. Only 50 applicants are accepted, and each must submit to a rigorous interview process to make sure that the fit is good for both parties. If you're ready to change your life, read more about the Kangaroo Millionaire Tribe by going to: www.kangaroomillionaire.com

• Strive to out-give everyone you encounter. Shower those you meet with encouragement, help, and a genuine offer of assistance. When you sense someone needs a listening ear, be there for them. Take the time to serve others and you will receive blessings beyond that which you or I can understand. That's what being a Kangaroo Millionaire is all about: realizing that there is no such thing as a "self-made" anything in life. We all need mentors and coaches who come alongside us and partner with us. We all need a Kangaroo to get us springing ahead to millionaire riches. Be someone else's Kangaroo. Find the 'Roo' in YOU!

SPECIAL FREE BONUSES
WORTH OVER $297!!!

To claim your $297 audio seminar training from Marc, send an email to freegift@marchrisko.com with "I'm Taking Action Now" in the subject line.

***

If you haven't already received Marc's popular e-book, *The 7 Fatal Mistakes Wannabe Millionaires Make* ($47 value), go to www.MarcHrisko.com and grab your copy now!

***

For news on Marc Hrisko's forthcoming teleseminars and live 3-day events, follow Marc on Twitter: http://twitter.com/MarcHrisko

***

Are you on Facebook? Who isn't? Stay in touch and send Marc a friend request on Facebook! Also, be sure to join the Kangaroo Millionaire Facebook Fan Page today!

ABOUT THE AUTHOR

One of the youngest members ever to be inducted into the Real Estate Hall of Fame, Marc Hrisko has been labeled a "rising star" and one of America's most dynamic wealth and entrepreneur strategists.

A top trainer for Robert Kiyosaki's "Rich Dad, Poor Dad" national seminars, Marc Hrisko's speeches and wealth-building seminars have been enjoyed by thousands of entrepreneurs in virtually every major city in the United States. In his role as a business coach, Marc has been responsible for helping launch the careers of some of the nation's top entrepreneurs.

Prior to his professional speaking and executive coaching career, Marc served 10 proud years as a firefighter and medic. Marc`s commitment to public service stems from his family's military legacy. Marc's father, a retired Navy Master Chief, is now an employee of Marc Hrisko International.

The Hrisko family's passion for service is now channeled through Marc Hrisko International's involvement in the Tidewater, Virginia, chapter of the Autism Society of America. Marc's strong support for autism research began when a fellow firefighter's child was diagnosed with autism.

Marc lives with his wife, Kym, and their two sons in Norfolk, Virginia.

NOTES

1. http://pubdb3.census.gov/macro/032006/perinc/new03_001.htm
2. http://www.ft.com/cms/s/0/a3794060-d1c3-11dd-bb61-000077b07658.html and http://www.globalissues.org/article/26/poverty-facts-and-stats
3. http://www.nytimes.com/2008/06/17/opinion/17brooks.html
4. Ibid.
5. Dr. Thomas J. Stanley, The Millionaire Next Door (New York: Pocket, 1998), 8.
6. http://www.reuters.com/article/idUSN1551763320081216
7. Felix Dennis, How to Get Rich: One of the World's Greatest Entrepreneurs Shares His Secrets (New York: Portfolio, 2008), xx.
8. http://moneycentral.msn.com/content/Savinganddebt/Managedebt/P150813.asp
9. Ibid. Also see: David Bach, The Automatic Millionaire Homeowner (New York: Broadway Books, 2005).
10. http://money.cnn.com/magazines/moneymag/money101/lesson9/index2.htm
11. Charles Fishman, "The War for Talent, Fast Company, September 11, 2008.
12. Laura Stack, Leave the Office Earlier (New York: Broadway Books, 2004).
13. http://www.thankgodimdyslexic.com.au/index.php?pgid=18
14. http://www.entrepreneur.com/magazine/entrepreneur/2008/

NOTES

november/198164.html

15. http://www.defendamerica.mil/articles/nov2004/a112904g.html

16. http://www.miamiherald.com/996/story/599578.html

17. http://blogs.wsj.com/independentstreet/2007/10/01/
growing-pains-cutting-off-deadbeat-clients/

18. http://www.entrepreneur.com/money/moneymanagement/
financialmanagementcolumnistpamnewman/article173108.html

19. http://blogs.wsj.com/independentstreet/2007/10/01/growing-
pains-cutting-off-deadbeat-clients/

20. http://www.financehotnews.com/small-business/overseas-
outsourcing-heats-up-again.html

21. Emily Maltby, "Overseas outsourcing heats up again," CNN
Money.com, November 11, 2008.

22. "Capitalize on expertise: learn how to make the most of your
valuable knowledge and advice when interacting with customers,"
PMA Magazine, December 1, 2006.

23. Bob Nightengale, "Baseball's bigger deal man; Agent Boras builds
empire by negotiating monster contracts for his clients," USA Today,
November 14, 2006, 1C.

24. http://www.cxoamerica.com/pastissue/article
asp?art=270126&issue=202

25. Helia Ebrahimi, "Rising stars rely on cash from homes: Second
mortgages fund many in Hot 100," Mail on Sunday, April 6, 2008, FB73.

26. Napoleon Hill. Think and Grow Rich. 291.

27. New Zealand Herald, September 24, 2007. http://www.lexisnexis.
com.proxy.lib.fsu.edu/us/lnacademic/results/docview/docview.
do?docLinkInd=true&risb=21_T5130854547&format=GNBFI&sort=REL
EVANCE&startDocNo=1&resultsUrlKey=29_T5130854550&cisb=22_T5
130854549&treeMax=true&treeWidth=0&csi=257912&docNo=13

28. http://www.time.com/time/magazine/article/0,9171,1858884,00.html

29. http://www.iff.com/internet.nsf/0/F7643DC9B354A53185256DAA006D3617

30. http://www.modernguitars.com/archives/003340.html

31. http://realtytimes.com/rtpages/20081017_hotmarket.htm

32. http://www.allbusiness.com/buying-exiting-businesses/franchising-franchises/1425-1.html

33. http://blog.guykawasaki.com/2007/01/ten_questions_w.html

34. http://www.forbes.com/2005/05/27/cx_sc_0527home.html

35. http://money.cnn.com/galleries/2007/real_estate/0704/gallery.stocks_v_realestate.moneymag/index.html

36. Gerber. 9.

37. 234

38. http://www.nytimes.com/2008/02/12/science/12tier.html?_r=1&scp=2&sq=NASCAR&st=nyt&oref=slogin

39. Steven Henry, August 16, 2008, pg. 25.

40. "Grandmaster Flash: Gordon Ramsay on global ambitions, a return to Scotland—and why he's turning his back on television," The Herald (Glasgow), May 17, 2008, 6.

41. http://www.wired.com/wired/archive/10.01/timeline.html

42. http://clusterstock.alleyinsider.com/2008/8/that-awesome-warren-buffett-cnbc-interview